THE HIDDEN WAR

ALSO BY R. A. HALDANE

THE HIDDEN WORLD

THE
HIDDEN
WAR

R. A. HALDANE

ST. MARTIN'S PRESS
NEW YORK

ROBERT HALE LIMITED
LONDON

© R. A. Haldane 1978
First published in Great Britain 1978
First published in the United States of America 1978

ISBN 0 7091 6486 6

Robert Hale Limited
Clerkenwell House
Clerkenwell Green
London EC1R 0HT

St. Martin's Press, Inc.,
175 Fifth Avenue
New York, N.Y. 10010

Library of Congress Catalog Card Number: 77-12279

Library of Congress Cataloging in Publication Data

Haldane, Robert A.
    The hidden war.

    Bibliography: p.
    Includes index.
    1. World War, 1939-1945—Cryptography. 2. World War,
1939-1949—Secret service. I. Title.
D810.C88H34   940.54'88   77-12279
ISBN 0-312-37197-7

Printed in Great Britain by
Lowe & Brydone Ltd., Thetford, Norfolk
Photoset and bound by
Weatherby Woolnough, Wellingborough, Northants.

CONTENTS

ILLUSTRATIONS

PICTURE CREDITS

Unless otherwise indicated all photographs were provided by
the Imperial War Museum.

Author's Note

There is now no former senior officer whom I could ask to write a foreword, as I was fortunate enough to secure for a previous book, so it may be as well if I provide the reader a short note about my experience in intelligence work over seven years, including World War II. I began with a period on cipher work from which I was later moved to Home Security War Room where I served as Officer of the Watch. In late 1941 I was appointed Personal Intelligence Staff Officer to Brigadier-General C. C. Lucas, Director of Intelligence, Home Security, and a member of the Home Defence Committee and various "working parties". In this last capacity, which I retained to the end of the war, I was responsible for keeping my chief posted with appreciations about the German Air Force on the Western Front, its strength, deployment and operations; also included in this were V1s (flying bombs), V2s (long-range rockets) and the threat, fortunately unrealized, of the atomic bomb. In 1943 I was additionally posted to a small intelligence directorate to take charge of the intelligence division, its *raison d'être*.

If the word "intelligence" carries any particular magic to outsiders, I can only say that it wears off quickly after appointment in office. In top secret intelligence work, whether it involves ciphers and codes or other duties, one works in little cells and often one is consulted without knowing the reason. On one occasion I was talking to the head of a small highly specialized directorate and we both found that we had been consulted about the plan to attack the Mohne and Eder dams but neither of us had realized it at the time. Likewise I was consulted by Combined Operations before the Dieppe raid and before Operation "Torch", the landing by the Allies on North-West Africa, also without knowing the purposes for which the information was required. Each man is a specialist in his own field and it is really only in that field that he can speak with authority. The man responsible for the distribution of intelligence may know little or nothing about the process of decrypting enemy signals or of the proportion received that are decrypted, while the cryptanalyst may not know how many of his readings are available in time to be of operational use at sea.

It can be said, therefore, that nobody is of himself qualified to write a book covering the wide field chosen for this work. He can consult papers available at the Office of Records and books by others who played their various parts in events, and in so doing he can put together a reasonably representative picture. He cannot, however, be confident that later revelations will not show some of his sources to be incorrect or his own deductions and conclusions to be ill-founded. For inevitably there is secret information which has not yet been revealed and, as I know, some that will forever remain secret.

R.A.H.

Acknowledgements

For permission to quote I am indebted to the following: David and Charles, *Secret Agents, Spies and Saboteurs* by Janusz Piekalkiewicz; William Collins Sons and Co., *The Gehlen Memoirs*; Peter Davies Ltd, *Crisis Convoy* by Vice-Admiral Sir Peter Gretton; Andre Deutsch Ltd, *The Schellenberg Memoirs* and *Philby, the Spy who Betrayed a Generation* by Bruce Page, David Leitch and Philip Knightley; the Hamlyn Publishing Group, *They Fought Alone* by Maurice Buckmaster; Her Majesty's Stationery Office, *The War at Sea* by Captain S. W. Roskill, RN; Hodder and Stoughton Ltd and Maximilian Becker, *The Game of the Foxes* by Ladislas Farago; Lieut-Colonel Knut Haukelid, *Skis Against the Atom*, Fontana-Collins; A. D. Peters Ltd, *Lord Chandos' Memoirs*, the Bodley Head; William Kimber and Co Ltd, *British Agent* by John Whitwell; Martin Secker and Warburg Ltd, *Codeword Direktor* by Heinz Hoehne; Weidenfeld and Nicolson Ltd, *Room 39, Naval Intelligence in Action 1939-45* by Donald McLachlan; *Inside S.O.E.* by E. H. Cookridge, Arthur Barker Ltd; Curtis Brown Ltd, *Anatomy of Spying* by Ronald Seth, Arthur Barker Ltd; and *Handbook for Spies* by Alexander Foote, published by Museum Press in 1953 and reprinted by permission of Pitman Publishing Ltd.

Every effort has been made to trace owners of copyright. If any have been accidentally omitted, I make my apologies.

My thanks are due to Mrs Wallace who deciphered my handwriting and in typing the text contributed to the checking of detail, and to Miss Janet Sandall for her painstaking help with revisions. It is a pleasure to record appreciation of work well done.

Notwithstanding these acknowledgements, for the text of this book I alone am responsible.

R.A.H.

Glossary of Terms

Alternates:	a choice of equivalents or alternatives for the same letter or numeral. See also *Suppression of frequencies.*
Cipher:	a disguised form of communication based on the alphabet; a whole book can be enciphered.
Ciphony:	enciphered telephony. The instrument used is known as a telephone scrambler.
Code:	a disguised form of communication based on a dictionary (e.g. a word may be represented by any group of letters or numerals, as the author pleases). No skill is required to decode, only access to the dictionary. A word not included in the dictionary cannot be encoded. In practice the word *code* is often used loosely to refer to ciphers.
Corrupt cipher:	an enciphered message in which there is a mistake in the enciphering.
Cryptanalysis:	the process of unravelling or breaking cryptosystems.
Cryptograms:	enciphered or encoded communications.
Cryptography:	literally, hidden writing.
Cryptology:	the hidden word. It includes spoken as well as written.
Cut-out:	a go-between or middle-man.
En clair:	the text of a message in ordinary language, usually referred to as the plain text.

Frequencies: the regular appearance of letters and words in average text. In English E is the commonest letter followed by T, A, O, N, R, I, S, H in that order; in Russian O is the most frequent, in Portuguese A. In English the six commonest words are *the, of, and, to, in* and *a* in that order. There are also frequencies in initial and final letters of words, and of names, and also of groups of letters.

Monoalphabetic cipher: a simple cipher based on a single alphabet (for example the letter A is always represented by the same letter).

Nulls: letters, words or numerals, not forming part of the text, introduced to complete a pattern (e.g. numerals grouped in fives).

One-time random pad: a pad bearing groups of random numerals; no two leaves are the same. Each leaf is used only once.

Polyalphabetic cipher: a cipher based on more than one alphabet (e.g. the letter A is represented by a variety of letters).

Substitution cipher: a cipher in which letters of the plain text are represented by other letters of the alphabet.

Suppression of frequencies: methods of disguising the more frequent letters, most commonly by the use of alternates but sometimes by omission of letters.

Transposition cipher: a cipher in which only the letters of the plain text are used but in a different order, as in an anagram.

ONE

ENTREE

Scarcely had the dust of the Second World War settled, and a bewildered and weary world had sat down to review the mess and think about repatriating some 15 million prisoners to their various homelands, and building things up again, than the first of a long series of memoirs and other war books made their appearance. Simultaneously, some of the leading Nazis got busy writing their memoirs in their cells at Nuremberg.

The flow of books began to accelerate. Some of those who had been employed in most secret work and had themselves been forbidden to keep diaries or to retain secret papers may have raised their eyebrows. They would probably not have been surprised later to learn that the diary of a general had fallen into Russian hands.[1] At all events the flow of revelations has continued, much of what was once secret is now public knowledge because there is no longer need for the same tight secrecy, and libraries periodically throw out some of the earlier works to make room for more recent ones.

Those with pre-war memories may recall a case that occasioned surprise in 1935. A Swiss journalist named Berthold Jacob was kidnapped by German agents and taken to Berlin. The cause of this was his well-informed revelations about the German Army, then being secretly built up again by Hitler. Where, Jacob was asked, had he got his information from? In surprise he replied that he had put it all together from published sources and, item by item, he named them. The incident provoked a diplomatic protest; the journalist was released and returned home to resume his labours.

With that recollection in mind, readers of *The Guardian*

(11th January 1975) will not have been surprised to learn, from a feature about a retiring official of the Central Intelligence Agency (CIA), that the store of intelligence of that well-known American service was principally put together, not from secret sources, but from diligently studied newspapers, periodicals, directories and other books, including the *Encyclopedia Britannica.* For the fact is that in the Western World little remains secret, although in this country we have the Official Secrets Act which exercises a restraining influence. In America there is no corresponding legislation and General Gehlen, a German officer who managed to shift his services from Nazi Germany to America, gave it as his opinion that in American intelligence circles "secret" meant "known to all" and "top secret" meant "known only to those who ask"*.[2] This rather sour comment is not, however, quite fair. But so far as the public are concerned, it is another matter and indeed the friends of Russia have been able to publish the names of CIA agents and where they have been posted. This contrasts strangely with a case that occurred in this country between the wars, when Compton Mackenzie was convicted and fined for a quite modest infringement of the Official Secrets Act.

Notwithstanding the restraint imposed in Britain by law, we have been favoured with books written not only by diplomats, senior members of the Armed Forces and interpreters, but also by men who served in our own Secret Intelligence Service (SIS, formerly known as MI6) or in the war-time Special Operations Executive (SOE) or in the *Maquis,* and we have even had the official history of SOE in France which has been claimed to be the only history of secret service work ever published by a British government. (In fact the activities of SOE had more in common with those of the Commandos than with espionage agents.) The book has not been popular in France, mainly because it was thought to exaggerate the part played by Britain. That criticism may have some justification, though it must be remembered that the Baker Street headquarters of SOE

---

* The highest category of secrecy in Britain was "Most Secret", but after America's entry into the war this was discontinued and the American designation "Top Secret" was adopted.

arranged training and provided arms, equipment, transport
and radio communications, as well as funds and, by no
means least, moral support when the going was hard. An
unanswerable criticism was the astonishing revelation that it
was believed in Baker Street that the ciphers being used by
the Free French to their agents could be read by the Germans,[3] but apparently SOE did not warn their Allies. When
Dewavrin, head of de Gaulle's Intelligence, read that, he
exploded with justifiable anger that, if that were really so, it
was surely criminal that no warning was given.

Of the productions of professional agents that of the
author calling himself John Whitwell is, I think, outstanding,
not only because he was evidently the ideal character – so
much so that he has been referred to as the "Father Brown
of British agents"[4] – but also because he wrote with such
charm. He is no longer alive but his little book is likely to
remain a classic. On quite a different and much lower level
we have had contributions from H. A. R. (Kim) Philby and
Kolon Molody, better known to us as Gordon Lonsdale, the
head of the Portland spy ring. Some remarkably revealing
products have come from the pens of distinguished jour-
nalists. *The Game of the Foxes* by Ladislas Farago who
unearthed from store the complete records of the Abwehr, is
an interesting addition to our knowledge.

The practice of an author criticizing another is unbecom-
ing but, if it is done with restraint, it cannot be objected to
when its purpose is to explain why a particular claim or
revelation has been found unacceptable. Even if the author
has been in "intelligence", it is no guarantee. Indeed that
elastic word is almost meaningless, for it covers anything
from a humble post in what might be called one of the fringe
services all the way up to espionage. Whether he has occupied a post in, for example, Reykjavik where he was posted
to keep an eye on what the Icelanders were doing or was one
of Cooper's Snoopers* or was in cipher work or in espionage,
no author is entitled to ride the high horse and claim that he
has discovered the truth, the whole truth and nothing but

* "Cooper's Snoopers" was the name given to those whose task it was to
listen to rumours and what people were saying and thinking, Duff
Cooper (later Viscount Norwich) then being Minister of Information.

the truth, because it overlooks one unquestionable truth which transcends all others. Because top secret work is top secret, it naturally follows that it does not lend itself to comprehensive written records. There were many highly secret matters and ideas during the war which quite properly were never set down on paper. Many of those secrets were once known only to people who are now dead, and they are therefore lost for ever. In this book I have told the story of secret communications which I have tried to show in perspective against the background of events; but it must be read subject to that overriding qualification. However, now that more than thirty years have elapsed, a certain amount of information has been released, in particular about the constructions devised, enabling us to read Enigma signals. The full story has not yet been told, but meanwhile enough is known to indicate that the history of the war may have to be rewritten.

Notwithstanding that we have had some interesting and instructive memoirs from men in senior positions, vanity has never been much of an ally of truth. Montgomery naturally enjoyed being credited with unfailing intuition in anticipating Rommel's moves. In fact he was being supplied in advance with the clear text of Rommel's orders of battle.[5]

Even within the confines of an individual's personal experience there may be matters about which he himself is unsure of the facts. To illustrate from my own experience, on one occasion I was called aside by Group-Captain Warburton and told that certain highly secret information would be coming through to me and that on no account should it be committed to writing. As I knew that at an earlier stage there had been consultation with the Free French to establish liaison and share certain information received from sources in France, it seemed a natural assumption that this intelligence which certainly originated in France was a product of those arrangements. Since then, however, I have wondered if it came from reading Enigma signals, a success of which at the time I was unaware.[6] Such experience of doubt must be common for, where intelligence of strict secrecy is concerned, it is practice to pass on to others only what they need to know and no more. As a result the right hand often does not

know what the left hand is doing. We shall not know the full
and official story of what has been called the Ultra secret for
a while, if we ever do. In dealing with secret work we cannot
regard any sources of information as really reliable, however
industrious the research. Even those who themselves were in
intelligence have only limited knowledge and may be incorrect. Memories are not infallible. Thus, Winterbotham
and Calvocoressi take rather different views about the contribution made by Ultra to the result of the Battle of Britain.
One day we may know which was right.

In this book I have drawn on Winterbotham's story of
the Ultra secret and a later work by Patrick Beesly,
supplemented by three talks by Calvocoressi on BBC radio.
The appearance of Winterbotham's book provoked a claim
on behalf of the Poles that they had been the first to read
Enigma signals. In 1937 they alone were indeed doing so, but
within two years changes in the Enigma machine defeated
them and they lost touch.[7] They did, however, provide both
the French and ourselves with Enigma machines and also
contraptions which they had used to read the earlier versions.
These helped us to develop our own sophisticated mechanism
which Winterbotham likens to a bronze goddess, a distinctive
term which I have adopted as convenient for reference. The
Poles who had been working on Enigma were in Southern
France when the Germans occupied it in 1942. They later fell
into the hands of the Gestapo but heroically gave nothing
away.[8]

In the text that follows I have simplified the story of the
bronze goddess. Set forth in full, so far as it is already known,
it would be somewhat technical. But we should bear in mind
that the term I have adopted refers to two devices. We might
regard them as Mark I which was electro-mechanical
(originally christened 'the bomb') and Mark II ('the colos-
sus') which was electronic. The first was not working before
the end of 1939, though full operation took time to develop;
the second dates from 1943.

*   *   *   *

Atttitudes of mind are much influenced by the fashion of
the day. Formerly an espionage agent was told, when his

services were engaged, that if he did well, he would get no recognition, and that, if he were caught, he would get no help. The agent who was convicted was the loneliest man in the world; his government disowned him and the best that he could hope for was a term in prison. But in recent years things have changed, and we are now accustomed to a sort of exchange and mart on the borders of East and West where periodically one espionage agent is exchanged for another. "What say we swap your Vladimir for our Willie?" we inquire – or perhaps it is the other way about. Like a couple of dealers we get together and, if the Russians think that the return of Vladimir to them would be more valuable than the return of Willie would be to us, the bargain is struck and the two men are exchanged. Willie is greeted with pleasure and vigorous handshakes, and his friends are delighted. We do not know what sort of reception Vladimir gets. Espionage is rarely mentioned in the Soviet press. So far as the public are given an official attitude to adopt, it seems to be disapproval.

Not only that, but there is nothing secret about these deals. Indeed agents who have been exchanged have been known afterwards to write their memoirs, telling of their experiences. At least one British agent has done so, and even a Russian one has had a book published in this country.

Others as well as British agents have been exchanged in this way; thus an American sky pilot was swapped for a Russian agent. Indeed it is not only between East and West that this strange market for bartering agents has come into being, nor when deals are agreed, is it always on a one-for-one basis. For we read how an Israeli agent, Wolfgang Lodz as he was known, and his wife were swapped, in a deal done with Cairo, for nine Egyptian generals, several hundred other officers and 5,000 other ranks. Another Israeli agent, Elie Cohen, on the other hand, was out of luck; he was caught by the Syrians who refused an offer from Israel of a million dollars for his release, and he was hanged in a public square in Damascus.[9] This market in espionage agents promises to provide interesting reading.

One of the more noteworthy passages in Schellenberg's memoirs is his comment that "the British Secret Service had a very long tradition and could count many of the ablest and

most intelligent of British people amongst its collaborators",
whereas German agents were regarded by their fellow
countrymen as suspicious characters, if not social outcasts.[10]
As Sir John Masterman observed in his story of German
agents "turned" to work for us, there are people with a
natural attraction to a life in the shadows where deceit and
intrigue are the main ingredients, spiced with danger. They
have a craving for adventure outside the law and are not
particular which side engages their services.[11] The distinction
of our own small *corps d'élite* stands in marked contrast to
many of the corresponding services of other countries. Those
that employ crooks must expect the standards that come
naturally to them.

When we come to consider the story of secret communications in the Second World War, we cannot really be
surprised that secrets have gone astray, and indeed the
wonder is that more did not do so, when we take into
account the casual attitude of some of our diplomatic
representatives. It is well known that during the war our
Ambassador to Turkey employed as his valet a spy known to
posterity as "Cicero" who obtained the Ambassador's key to
the safe, photographed secret documents and sold them to
the Germans. What is not so well known is that during the
Thirties the same diplomatic dignitary, then our Minister to
the Baltic States, employed as his footman a young man
known as Toni who might not have attracted the attention
that he did, had he not been notorious as Riga's highest paid
male prostitute. Though these personal activities were common knowledge, they were not known to our Minister. The
local Abwehr agent pressed the footman to work for the
Germans. It was then – and indeed remained – the Minister's
practice to take to his bedroom suite his despatch box containing secret papers and his keys. Toni got hold of the keys
on one occasion, made a wax impression and afterwards
adopted the practice of opening the safe and photographing
the papers. The British agent, Leslie Nicholson ("John
Whitwell") warned the Minister who, however, continued
to employ the footman.[12] So Nicholson informed the Foreign
Office. They, too, did nothing. In 1934 the Minister was
posted to Teheran as Ambassador and subsequently to

Ankara where he served during the war years. After his departure from Riga, his successor to that post continued the employment of the same footman. Such were the standards of security, if such they can be called, during the Thirties when Britain slept.

When diplomatic representatives do not care whether their footmen are spies in the service of other powers, and the Foreign Office does not care either, we must truly be what the Americans call "suckers" for spies. One would expect that the man would be immediately dismissed, that the lock of the safe would be changed and that steps would be taken to see that it was frequently changed thereafter.

In Berlin our Ambassador's indiscreet telephone conversations with the Foreign Office in the years immediately before war broke out knew no bounds; he had only to be lured to the tapped telephone for the Germans to learn all that they wanted to know.[13] These conversations removed the last chances our ciphers had of remaining secret, for they inevitably provided tin-openers. In Rome our Ambassador's behaviour was no less extraordinary, the embassy safe being visited once a week by an Italian agent on the staff over a number of years. Nothing was done to tighten security, even when a diamond tiara belonging to the Ambassador's wife was stolen.[14] The agent who was not stupid knew a good bargain when he saw one and not only disposed of the tiara but also did well for himself by selling copies of the secret documents to the Russian Embassy as an unauthorized sideline. Ciano happily recorded in his diary that he was reading every British signal, but added that he wondered if other people were not equally good at the game. He at least had his head screwed on, which is more than could be said for our ambassadors who seemed to be indifferent to the requirements of security.

During the war Sir William Stephenson, Director of British Security Co-ordination, an Anglo-American secret service, had occasion to visit Lima where the British Ambassador invited him to lunch and in front of his servants and other guests said: "So you have come down here to do a secret service job, have you?"

Not all our ambassadors and ministers have been indifferent to the presence of enemy agents on their staff, however, and one who took exception to it was D'Arcy Osborne, Minister to the Holy See; advised that one of his staff named Livio was in the employment of the Italian Secret Service, he did at least dismiss him on the advice of SIS.[15] (Osborne held office from 1936 to 1947, and was Britain's only diplomatic representative in enemy territory throughout the war.)

If diplomats are sometimes as casual and indifferent about security as this, it is not perhaps surprising that indiscretions occur elsewhere. Shortly before the Dieppe Raid, a MI5 man, doing his rounds in the Shoreham-Newhaven area, found a naval officer in a public house, holding in his hands his operational orders; he had the officer arrested.[16] Before "Torch", a copy of the plan was found in a Whitehall gutter.

But that was nothing to the catalogue of carelessness in the last few days before D-Day, when Overlord* briefings blew out of an open window in Whitehall, a lorryload of invasion maps spilled out on to the road and a briefcase containing complete Overlord plans was found in a train at Exeter.[17]

It is impossible to estimate what proportion of successful reading of others' ciphers owes something to external influences, but it is certainly far from negligible and, if one made a guess at 50 per cent, it might be an underestimate. Diplomatic offices are to espionage agents what lamps are to moths. Even where a cipher in the safe of an embassy or legation has not actually been photographed by an agent who has managed to gain entry, an office cleaner may have seen a cipher machine and be able to describe its appearance. Confidential waste which one might think it no more than elementary prudence to burn on the premises was stolen by the sack load, sometimes openly carried out in laundry baskets and sold; this was far from uncommon. Clues may, however, come to hand rather than be actively sought. A merchant ship in the early stages of a long voyage may receive the first signal in a new code before reaching port and collecting a copy and in such a case ask that the signal be repeated in the old code which may have been

* "Overlord" was the code name for the operation after the landing in Normandy; the code name for the Channel crossing was "Neptune".

broken in part or whole. A diplomat may present a note from his government on the strength of instructions received in cipher; a comparison of the intercept and the plain text will provide a tin-opener. Boris Hagelin expressed the view that the greatest risk to ciphers arose from external circumstances of one kind or another.[18] But reckless use of ciphers is surely a greater one; a second rate cipher sparingly used is more secure than a better one that is used too much. On occasion warning has been given direct that a system was known to the enemy; thus, it was Admiral Darlan who told Admiral Leahy, then American Ambassador to the Vichy Government, that their diplomatic signals were being read by the Germans. It is often safer to conclude that a cipher has been read rather than to record that it has been unravelled by cryptanalysts, though this is not to underestimate the importance of the part they play. It is vital, as the story of the Battle of the Atlantic demonstrates.

The successful reading of the enemy's Enigma, the product of a remarkable feat of cryptanalysis, was far and away the most important achievement of its kind in our history, so much so that information was accorded a special category of secrecy of its own, called "Ultra". It was even more precious than was the reading by the Americans of the Japanese cipher, Purple; electro-mechanical aids notwithstanding, the breaking of Enigma was a feat of great skill, for the permutations ran into millions of millions. There were numbers of Enigma keys used simultaneously; we read many signals but not all.[19]

For the duration of the war, Enigma was used throughout the German High Command: Hitler used it, Goering, Raeder, Doenitz, Keitel and Kesselring – all the men at the top – used it. The store of information amassed from reading their signals was of immense importance. This vital asset was in use by April 1940. When France fell two months later, Germany was astride Europe from the Arctic to the Pyrenees and Britain stood alone. The miracle of Dunkirk was begun on 27th May and completed on 3rd June; 366,131 men were brought to this country (224,686 British and 141,445 French or Belgian) in 222 ships of the Royal Navy and 665 other craft, mostly quite small, while the sea was mercifully calm.

In such circumstances ability to read various signals between Hitler and his senior officers – none surely more garrulous than Goering – was an essential defensive asset, for Hitler expected Britain to surrender. Nearly a year later Rudolph Hess, probably on his own initiative, flew over, apparently hoping to persuade us;* perhaps his mind had already begun to go.

During the Battle of Britain, when the German Air Force sought to reduce defences to a state where invasion of the island could be put into operation, Dowding, then Air Officer Commanding-in-Chief, Fighter Command, had to keep the Ultra secret to himself. As has been said, it was indeed he who won the Battle of Britain and he who then protected the security of Ultra.[21] This contrasted with the enemy's intelligence services which, for the most part, could not compete with ours; for in July 1940 Keitel could report only that German intelligence about Britain's defences was meagre and unreliable.[22]

On 7th September 1940, London suffered its first big night attack by the GAF.† These attacks continued without a break until 3rd November when there was a pause. Knowing what he did of the enemy's intentions, Dowding was the better able to defeat a numerically superior force; between 10th July, when day attacks began, and the end of October, 1,089 enemy aircraft were destroyed.[23]

Whatever Ultra information Dowding had at his disposal, he rightly kept it to himself; certainly he did not reveal its source to his staff. At that stage security was about as tight

* On the night of 10th May 1941 German bombers made their heaviest attack on London. While this battering was in its later stages, an alert Air Intelligence Officer warned the Officer of the Watch at Home Security War Room that a single fighter aircraft was crossing the North Sea from Germany towards Scotland. The remaining hours of darkness were limited and such an aircraft would not then have had either the time or the fuel to make the return flight as well; the conclusion was that the visitor was travelling on a single ticket. The Officer of the Watch asked to be kept posted and was astonished to learn later that the visitor was none other than Rudolph Hess who had hoped to see the Duke of Hamilton at his home in Scotland. Hess was interned for the remainder of the War.[20]

† For the sake of security this abbreviation was used in intelligence appreciations in preference to "Luftwaffe".

as it could have been. This problem was not confined to direct attacks on Britain. It applied equally to the Battle of the Atlantic, to the war in North Africa and elsewhere. How far down the line could the secret be allowed to go? Hardly at all. We had to make use of our precious treasury of knowledge without risking its own security. A balance had to be struck; we later extended the circulation somewhat.

As we shall see, the Americans were faced with the same problem arising from their ability to read the Japanese cipher, Purple, in which the Japanese had as much faith as the Germans had in Enigma – in fact even more, for when the Germans learnt through an agent that the Americans were reading Purple signals and advised their allies, the Japanese were so cocky about their cipher which they regarded as impossible to break, that they refused to believe it.

*   *   *   *

There are differences in the amount of information made public since the war about the performances of cipher staff. In some cases this has been because records fell into others' hands; even so, not all nations go to the same lengths to make a mystery of it. Are the Germans any the worse off because other countries now know how their services performed? It is difficult to see why they should be. It is all past history now. Yet it remains to be seen if anything will be officially released about the performance of our crypt-analysts; there may of course be good reasons for with-holding it. But no doubt, too, there are occasions when reasons are non-existent. As Dusko Popov comments, bureaucratic lethargy and the easy way out of taking no action have perpetuated secrets that no longer have a genuine *raison d'être*.[24] There have been occasions when we seem to have taken security to remarkable lengths. Thus we learn that at one stage of the war the officer in charge of defence against U-boats informed Admiral of the Fleet Sir Dudley Pound that he had received advice from the Director of Naval Intelligence that the Tracking Room had been "blinded", a thinly disguised way of explaining that the

Germans had changed the system and that their signals were no longer being read. Since new systems, or existing ones in which major changes are made, are not broken overnight, and the Germans obviously knew of the change, one wonders why any disguise at all was necessary, the more so as the information was for the First Sea Lord. One wonders indeed what objection there could have been to officially making it public before now.

Vice-Admiral Sir Peter Gretton has expressed his views in straightforward terms. "Official policy," he writes, "is still, wrongly I believe, to keep this side of the war effort a deadly secret and it is therefore impossible to get any authentic information."[25] He goes on to point out that it was known that the submarine *U 111* had been captured intact with much valuable intelligence material; many officers and men knew what had happened as well as some of the survivors from sunken merchant ships. But even the official historian was unaware of the event until after he had completed his history. Since the publication of Gretton's book a limited amount of information has been made public.

In some ways we are remarkably careless; there were enough hair-raising examples on the eve of D-Day. We do not seem to exercise consistency or judgement when discriminating between circumstances which demand the tightest security measures and others when the release of official historical information could no longer compromise security.

In the official history of the war at sea we are provided with a long and detailed record, which is occasionally brilliant in style, particularly in the closing passages of the final volume. But we are not told much about how we fared reading enemy signals, and at times we get the impression that the author was denied access to knowledge but felt bound to say something. Such passages as were permitted for public consumption are not distinguished by daring. Thus, after stating that the enemy made "substantial penetration" of our ciphers, the author goes on to say, "the reader should not of course assume that the British were meantime idle in achieving the opposite purpose", [26] which gives little enough away. This unenlightening passage refers to 1942 in the last nine months of which we were – on all the evidence available – completely baffled by the system used by the U-boats, while the enemy's penetration of British signals was practically total long before the end of the year.

Though we are, in the main, thrown back on unofficial histories and other contributions, we are fortunately well served. I have made use of more than a score of excellent books on the war at sea, several by senior serving officers of the Royal Navy, one by McLachlan and a more recent one by Beesly, both of Naval Intelligence, one comprehensive work by Rear-Admiral Morison of the US Navy, and five by notable German writers: Raeder and Doenitz, von der Porten and Frank (both on Doenitz's staff at U-boat Command), and Busch who commanded a U-boat. There is also Irving's revealing book with German records of unravelling our systems.

There are a number of contributors to the story of SOE, and of their works I have concentrated principally on fifteen, the comprehensive European history of Cookridge being outstanding. (The official history is confined to France.) There is a smaller variety of works dealing with Russian espionage, the Rote Kapelle and Sorge in Japan. We have even had revelations by men who distinguished themselves in our own secret services, in particular, Sir John Masterman, formerly of MI5, and our SIS agent, Leslie Nicholson. Always at our elbow, too, is Kahn's history of code breaking. There are many works which contribute only here and there to the story of secret communications but do so usefully.

If there are those who would question the inclusion of Hutton's information about the training of Russian agents, I would make three points in favour of adopting his material. In the first place Sir Robert Bruce Lockhart who wrote a foreword to one of that author's books on the subject would certainly not have done so, had he thought it bogus, and in the second place Sir Percy Sillitoe, formerly head of our Security Service (better known to the public under its war-time name of MI5) would not have expressed an opinion of that training. In addition similar information has at one time or another reached the American Embassy in Moscow, though it cannot be accepted as substantiated fact. But how much about Russia's secret services could be so designated? It should be remembered that, when Alexander Foote's book, *Handbook for Spies,* was first published, it was thought by a number of people to have been contrived, whereas we have all learnt to recognize that in fact it was entirely genuine. Foote's failure to reveal that Roessler was the identity of "Lucy" was due to the fact that Roessler was then alive; it was not an attempt to create a fictional character.

But of some of the works to be found in my sources of information it is reasonable to be wary in accepting at least some of what they say. Gehlen, a faceless man if ever there was one (indeed he wished so to be), wrote his memoirs which have themselves been described as faceless. There was certainly a great deal that he did not say. More to the point, some of what he did say is open to question; in particular, his claim that Martin Bormann went over to the Russians is decidedly improbable, the evidence being that he was killed in the last days of the collapse of the Nazi regime.

Nor is the shifty Schellenberg to be swallowed readily. Though he was at one time in charge of counter-espionage and later of the reorganization of Germany's foreign intelligence service, effectively he was probably never much more than the halitosis of the Gestapo Second XI. Rather naturally, he barely mentions the concentration camps or the massacre of the Jews. He has little enough to say of the unsuccessful plot to kill Hitler in July 1944; and of course he does not tell us if, as we believe, he was the bright spark who advised that the Casablanca Conference in January 1943* was to take place in the White House.[27] The omissions, however, matter less than the inclusions. Thus, Schellenberg tells us that Moscow's agent, Trepper, was moving about France, transmitting first from one place and then from another, always on the move, at a time when the evidence is that he was not in possession of a wireless transmitter. Nonetheless, Schellenberg's memoirs are interesting and

---

* We are told that a Spanish Secret Service agent got advance wind of this meeting between Churchill and Roosevelt and sent enciphered advice to that effect to Berlin where, however, it was thought that the word "Casablanca" should be read as two words, being the code name for the White House.

there are passages that fit known facts and are informative. His career was over by the time he was thirty-five; he was only forty-two when he died.

It would have been interesting if we had been left something from the pen of Canaris, though how far he would have opened out we may wonder. He was appointed in 1934 to take charge of the German Intelligence Service; he seems originally to have had an open mind about Hitler's régime. Subsequently Himmler and his Gestapo took over from him, but Canaris remained in service elsewhere till his dismissal in 1944. His loyalty was doubted and he was imprisoned for some months; he was executed with the maximum cruelty* only shortly before Hitler's suicide.

From what one gathers, Canaris was by no means an unpleasant character and he certainly had none of the hardness of Heydrich. He is credited with having forestalled Hitler's plans to murder the two French Generals, Weygand and Giraud, and five other French Generals.[29] It has been suggested that he may have worked for the Allies[30] but, in the sense of being used by SIS, that seems doubtful. It may well be that he had become disenchanted with Nazi rule even before the war[31] and it is likely that, as the tide began to turn and he regarded Germany's defeat as inevitable, he decided to trim his sails and do nothing to delay it. He was not the only German to turn against Hitler. Like others who did so, he has sometimes been described as a traitor, and in a sense he was. But such ready condemnation is not really apposite. In this country we have not had experience of cruel autocracy and let us hope we never shall. But if we had, would we be content to say: "This life is a horror. Let us leave it to our children to inherit and do nothing about it"? It is one thing to record that Canaris and others were disloyal to Hitler and his odious régime; it is another to be self-righteous about it.

* Hitler liked to have his victims strangled with piano wire, usually strung from meat hooks, death taking up to twenty minutes. According to Colonel Hinchley, Canaris was slowly strangled in this way, cut down and revived and then strangled fatally. Through the keyhole of his neighbouring cell, Colonel Lunding, head of Danish Military Intelligence, saw Canaris taken naked to the execution yard, having already been knocked about.[28]

This insularity is also to be found in our relations with France. It is well known and beyond question that de Gaulle was a prickly character, difficult to get on with, and much of our rather unhappy relations with him may be attributed to that. But it was not wholly one sided. That SOE did a first-class job and a most heroic one is not to be denied, but at times political direction was not the most adroit. Since the aim of the Free French was the liberation of their own country, they might have looked for more of a hand in the shaping of operations. Nor were they alone in that predicament, for Norwegian relations with Britain at one stage were virtually frozen, and almost the same could be said of the Dutch.

In some quarters the prejudice persisted for some time against the practice of breaking and reading other people's ciphers, and even some of our senior officers thought it was not really cricket to read Hitler's secret orders.[32] Indeed it was not; we were not playing cricket. Espionage may be acceptable to some people who look upon it as an adventure, and our own agents (who would not like to be referred to as "spies") were the *crème de la crème* of their profession and could be taken to the most exclusive and fastidious clubs. But when it came to stooping to read other people's communications, it was to some people something that just was not done. Most, like Eisenhower, had open minds and recognized its immense value,[33] and probably by the end of the war only the really obtuse still nursed their prejudice. One has only to study the history of the Battle of the Atlantic or, for that matter, the Battle of Britain, to appreciate how essential to our survival were the services of our cipher experts, both those constructing our own systems and those unravelling the enemy's.

In the hidden war, let it be remembered, the enemy succeeded in breaking the telephone scrambler* used by

---

* A telephone scrambler is a device fixed to a telephone instrument; it can be used only when speaking to someone likewise equipped. The device "scrambles" speech so that during transmission it is unintelligible to anyone listening in but is normal to the two talking to one another. There are various technical means of "scrambling". The process is known as "ciphony", a combination of cipher and telephony.[34]

Churchill and Roosevelt in their frequent talks on the tran-
satlantic telephone. It was when, through skilful research, the
enemy found the way to listen in to one of these conversations that they became aware that the Italians had secretly
approached the Allies about a separate armistice. They at
once set about murdering senior Italian officers then unfortunate enough to be with them and also took over Allied
prisoners who had been in Italian hands. It was through
knowledge of this that the Allies realized that, as General
Marshall had feared and had warned Roosevelt, the enemy
had unravelled that particular type of scrambler. Another
was brought into use and was never broken. What would
have happened, we may well wonder, had that change not
been made and the enemy had learnt in advance where the
Second Front was to be launched? The answer was provided
by the man responsible for the planning of operations,
Lieutenant-General Morgan, who warned that if the enemy
obtained as much as forty-eight hours advance knowledge of
the assault area, the chances of success would be small and
that any longer meant certain defeat for the Allies.[35]

The hidden war may not be the story of man at his best
and noblest, but that is beside the point. The service was
essential to the success of operations. It is not before time
that the attempt was made to put that service in the scales
of fortune and to judge to what extent it tipped them. That
is what I have sought to do in this book. Whether the
balance I have struck is correct is for others to judge.

In an appendix to the text of this book I have provided an
outline timetable of main events of the war. Complex
inter-related influences make it difficult to link much of
this detail directly with the reading of ciphers and codes. An
exception is the Battle of the Atlantic where, if one allows for
the small number of U-boats in the early stages and for the
use of direction-finders in the final stage, and especially for
periods when Hitler disrupted the conflict, the direct
influence of fortunes in the hidden war of ciphers and codes
can be closely related to those of the battle itself.

The cipher clerk who has to encipher outgoing signals and
decipher incoming ones is not a distinguished mathematician
but an ordinary person who has learnt his job. In fact

prisoners of war made use of their own systems, elementary though some of them may have been.[36] Given command of plain words, it should be possible to explain how most ciphers work and, in the case of complex electronic cipher machines, to provide an explanatory outline. I have sometimes doubted whether it is sufficient to copy out a real example as a demonstration. If the author devises his own, he applies his mind and is the better able to explain the processes involved; and that is what I have done, providing simple examples.

A book of this nature requires that adequate sources should be provided; and in certain cases where new ideas are advanced, because I have linked one acceptable fact with another and drawn conclusions, for example in the story of the Battle of the Atlantic, I have provided plentiful sources. Sources, however, show no more than where to look. Thus Cadogan's diary contains passages by Professor Dilks who edited it, and he in turn refers to other sources, in one case no fewer than seven; nor are these to be regarded as ultimate sources, for there is much that is now general knowledge among cryptographers. Accordingly in many cases I could have given several sources; the ones given, however, provide variety and should be helpful to the reader.

For the benefit of those who are new to this subject I have included a short and simple glossary of the few technical terms used. If they read this first, they will find no difficulty in following the main text.

TWO

THE LONG NIGHT
The Battle with the U-boats

At eleven-fifteen on the morning of 3rd September 1939, Neville Chamberlain, the Prime Minister, announced to the nation that Britain was at war with Germany. France's declaration followed at five o'clock that afternoon. The period between that date and 10th May 1940, when the enemy suddenly struck at the Low Countries and then into France, became known as the *Sitzkrieg* or phoney war. Phoney it may well have seemed to most people, as General Gamelin's troops in the Maginot Line and other French and British troops remained at action stations, while the daily *communiqué* from the Western Front announced with unfailing regularity: "There is nothing to report." Since most of the public knew scarcely anything of what was happening at sea, the conclusion was that, so far as Britain and France were concerned, it was a remarkably uneventful start to the war. Leaflets were dropped on Germany, inviting the people not to fight; and a naughty Lord Chamberlain lifted his ban on the music hall song "Even Hitler had a Mother". It was difficult to believe that a serious war had really started.

But from the day when the declaration was made, there was nothing phoney about the war at sea. In mid-August a few U-boats moved out into the Atlantic and took up waiting positions. Meanwhile there was the usual average of some 2,500 British merchant ships on the high seas going about their business. Only ten hours after the declaration of war, the 13,500-ton liner *Athenia*, homeward bound and about two hundred miles west of Ireland, was torpedoed by one of these U-boats and sunk with the loss of 112 lives. She had, we are told, been mistaken for an auxiliary cruiser.[1] Three days later a merchant ship fired on a U-boat.[2] During what was called the "phoney war", over 400 merchant ships* were sunk at a

* All figures for merchant ships sunk include British, Allied and neutral.

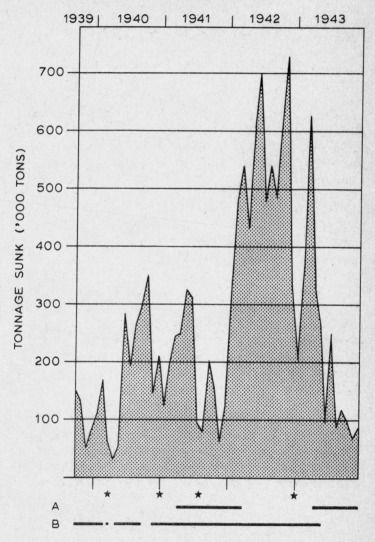

MERCHANT SHIPPING SUNK BY U-BOATS
1939-1943

★ Periods when Hitler's orders interrupted U-Boat operations.

A Periods when N.I. are believed to have read German signals.

B Periods when B-Dienst are believed to have read British signals.

cost of seventeen U-boats, and in addition the *Courageous* was sunk with a heavy loss of life. On 14th October the *Royal Oak* was torpedoed at her moorings in Scapa Flow, and in December the *Graf Spee* which had just sunk the *Doric Star* in the South Atlantic was herself scuttled at the conclusion of the Battle of the River Plate. During this period, too, six destroyers and three submarines were lost.[3]

From the first day of hostilities the war at sea was ceaselessly fought, often in darkness, over millions of square miles, and by the end of it the huge merchant tonnage of 14,687,231 (2,828 ships) had been sunk by U-boats,[4] by far the greater part of it in the North Atlantic.* In the history of naval warfare the Battle of the Atlantic was unique in its scale, its intensity and its duration. Fatal casualties among merchant seamen were high; one estimate gives 22 per cent[5] and another 17 per cent[6] (they are based on different estimates of the total number of merchant seamen) compared with 9.3 per cent for the Royal Navy, 9 per cent for the Royal Air Force and 6 per cent for the Army. Whatever the rate, it would have been considerably higher but for the rescue ships which had the unenviable task of remaining stationary to pick up survivors, sitting ducks for the U-boats.[7]

For Britain the Battle of the Atlantic, principally the North Atlantic, was the crucial struggle, and the critical phase of it did not end till the spring of 1943. If Hitler had known something of naval warfare or had taken the advice of those who did, the war would have taken a different course. "The only thing that ever really frightened me", Churchill afterwards recorded, "was the U-boat peril." He added that it would have been wise for the Germans to stake everything on it. In the event it was in the Battle of the Atlantic, as much as anywhere, that the war was won.

But before reviewing this long-drawn-out and desperate struggle and the parts played in it by British and enemy cipher services, we should look back to the pre-war years

---

* The total losses of merchant shipping in all areas and from all forms of enemy action amounted to 21,570,720 tons (5,150 ships). The North Atlantic and United Kingdom waters accounted for 82.9 per cent of the tonnage sunk.

from which there were relevant lessons to be remembered now and always.

The convoy system was first used during the Napoleonic wars. It was revived during the First World War, though neither Admirals Jellicoe or Beatty were in favour of it. During the Thirties no effort was made to see that we were properly equipped to make use of it again, notwithstanding the looming menace of Nazi Germany. In 1939 Britain had 150 destroyers of which half had seen action in the First World War and were held in reserve, and there were also some vessels for coastal patrols and a handful of sloops. The low fuel endurance of these destroyers was a handicap; and in fact escorts which could make the whole crossing of the Atlantic did not become feasible till the summer of 1941.[8] It must be borne in mind that the direct distance across the Atlantic was not that covered by an escort vessel completing the crossing, for it had to zig-zag almost continuously and at times went off on searches after suspected U-boats or rounding up stragglers.[9]

This quite inadequate number of vessels was all we had, to look after some 3,000 ocean-going merchant ships and 1,000 coasters. Two months before the outbreak of war the first escort vessels of the type to be known as corvettes were ordered, at that stage contemplated for coastal duties; these did not begin to appear till the summer of 1940. RAF Coastal Command had a few squadrons of aircraft with a range of just over 500 miles or less than a third of the direct route across the Atlantic between this country and Canada. Their range was later developed and the enemy noted that by the summer of 1942 it had been extended to 800 miles.[10]

It is customary and often correct to attribute responsibility for bad judgement and blunders to our political leaders. But it is a fact that in the First World War the insistence on using the convoy system came from Lloyd George and Maurice Hankey, while in the Second World War Chiefs of Staff showed little enthusiasm for, and even open hostility towards, irregular warfare, and the Commandos and Special Operations Executive came into being on Churchill's edict. (In fact SOE was first visualized by Chamberlain.) Some of the Chiefs of Staff were remarkably blinkered at times. Thus,

Air Marshal Harris of Bomber Command was against re-
leasing even one Liberator to Coastal Command, notwithstanding that it was widely acknowledged, not only in naval
circles, that the presence of a single aircraft over a convoy
greatly hampered U-boat operations.[11] As Vice-Admiral
Gretton has observed, if the Battle of the Atlantic had been
lost, there would have been no import of metals or aviation
spirit for our bombers[12] and, he could have added, the war
would have been lost.

Germany began the war with fifty-seven U-boats of which
not more than twenty-seven were of the ocean-going type; on
average about a third of that force was on patrol at any one
time. By comparison our own strength in submarines was
fifty-eight. The ocean-going U-boats had a maximum surface
speed of seventeen knots and carried fourteen torpedoes; they
had fuel capacity for 10,000 miles.

When the convoy system was started, the inadequacy of
escort vessels restricted the number of convoys. Ships that
were either fast (which meant with a maximum speed exceeding fifteen knots) or too slow (having a maximum speed
of less than nine knots) were excluded. Exceptionally fast
ships like the *Queen Mary* and the *Queen Elizabeth* which could
race any U-boat with plenty to spare – though that was no
guarantee of safety – plied to and fro, carrying
no fewer than 15,000 troops each trip without mishap.[13] The
Aquitania, Mauritania, and *Île de France* which in 1940 was
requisitioned together with the *Nieuw Amsterdam,* also had
maximum speeds exceeding twenty-eight knots and looked
after themselves. Some of those sailing independently may
have been glad of the freedom to sail as and when it suited
them without having to wait for the formation of the next
convoy, but the risk was the greater, as the demands of
insurance underwriters demonstrated.[14]

The Western Approaches escort force was divided between
the ports of Liverpool, Greenock, Londonderry and later
Belfast, principally the first two. Ships in convoy sailed in
columns; there might be four or five in a column. Columns
sailed about 1,000 yards apart and ships within the same
column about 400 yards apart. A convoy might occupy a
total area of about five square miles. (To put things in

perspective, the North Atlantic is about 13 million square miles and the South Atlantic a little less.) In 1943, on the advice of Professor Blackett, the number of ships per convoy was increased and could be as many as 150.[15]

At night a strict black-out was observed. If escort commanders received Admiralty signals about the positions of U-boats and darkness had then fallen, executing evasive action raised problems of communication.[16] Radio telephone could be picked up by the enemy and therefore entailed encoding and decoding when time might be precious, and steam whistles were inadequate and semaphore and code-flags no use at all. Signal searchlight was confined to daylight when the shutters of the lamps would clatter away. An innovation was forthcoming when an American telephone handset known as TBS (talks between ships) was brought into use, working through loudspeakers on the bridge, though as all ships were on the same frequency, one ship might unintentionally jam another.[17]

Sometimes convoys became scattered by fog, snow or heavy seas; and, in a storm with no moon, ships might be separated from their escorts by dawn.[18] On one occasion some ships found themselves in one of our own minefields,[19] and sometimes a "lame duck" would lag behind, unable to keep up with the convoy due to some cause such as poor coal.[20]

The fortunes of ships attacked varied. Those carrying timber might survive, at least for a time, though they could create a risk of a collision. Thus, on one convoy the *Carsbreck* with a cargo of timber was torpedoed but continued to stay afloat.[21] Ships carrying iron ore on the other hand went down quickly. Cargoes of high explosives and oil were of course particularly vulnerable and, when hit, could be a danger to other ships nearby.

After the attack on Denmark the Icelandic Government invited the British Government to establish a base there, to prevent the island falling into Nazi hands; and on 8th May 1940 the *Glasgow* and the *Berwick* left Greenock, carrying Royal Marines who on arrival rounded up all the Germans in Iceland for shipment to this country.[22] Thereafter convoy routes curled north towards Iceland where aircraft patrols were established, and then south towards Nova Scotia or the Irish Sea. A hazard created by this routing was the risk of icebergs at night.[23] Aircraft patrols operated by RAF Coastal Command and the Royal Canadian Air Force provided help but until the range of aircraft had been considerably increased, there remained an unpatrolled area in mid-Atlantic which, for most of this prolonged struggle, was from 800 to 600 miles wide. (In fact the gap might be regarded as having been closed in 1943, when Portugal granted the Allies the use of air bases in the Azores, but by then the Battle of the Atlantic had been decided.) This gap was known as "The Black Pit" and a map showing points at which ships were sunk is heavily dotted in this area.

During this struggle various inventions played their parts, efficacy being developed with experience. The two that contributed most were almost certainly radar and direction-finders; centimetric radar and high-frequency direction-finders were notable inventive achievements. Others were, however, also noteworthy. (1) Asdic, the brain-child of Professor Jock Anderson,[24] was a chemical discharge which created bubbles which returned the echo when detecting a U-boat that was submerged; these echoes were made audible through earphones or loud-speakers. The range of asdic was, however, less than that of radar and more restricted in high seas. Radar was the complement to asdic, as it could detect U-boats on the surface. (2) The gnat was an acoustic type of torpedo the hydrophones of which attracted it to ships' propellers. Our answer to it was (3) the foxer, a device which attracted the acoustic torpedo and was towed astern of ships. The enemy in turn produced (4) the zig-zag torpedo and (5) the depth torpedo charged with a magnetic detonator which broke the backs of ships, causing them to sink quickly. To the torpedo menace we answered with (6) degaussing cables* which from March 1940 were fitted to ships in such quantities that it amounted to many thousands of miles of it during the first two years of the war.[25] We also produced (7) the hedgehog, a multi-barrelled

---

* Degaussing (demagnetizing) cables reduced the natural magnetic field of a ship's steel hull so that the mechanism of a magnetic mine was not set in motion.

mortar, mounted on the forecastle. It fired twenty-four depth bombs 250 yards ahead of the estimated position of a U-boat, the bombs exploding on impact. The enemy introduced (8) the snorkel, an air-intake and diesel exhaust mast which enabled a U-boat just below the surface to recharge batteries at periscope depth. We produced (9) snowflake, a rocket that burst at 1,000 feet into a brilliant illuminant. There were both smoke screens and mines, inherited from 1918, the latter soon to be developed into the magnetic type.

When the Second World War broke out, radar and high frequency direction-finders were still in course of development. A refinement of radar was the plan position indicator (PPI) which provided a visual presentation of the area round a ship on which any object detected was shown by a spot of light. But it is not surprising that, in the opinion of one of our distinguished officers, direction-finders played as great a part in the defeat of the U-boats as did radar.[26]

In the early stages the enemy might be unaware of a new detecting device like asdic,[27] but probably every device invented by both the Allies and the enemy soon became known to both.

At the outbreak of hostilities the inadequate supply and range of suitable escort vessels was not the only major disadvantage under which we laboured. For a worse one was the cryptanalytic skill of Beobachtung-Dienst (B-Dienst henceforth) which was the smallest of the various cipher and code services of the enemy; it was virtually independent of the others, answerable to Doenitz, then Flag Officer, U-boats, and comprised a team of fifty cryptanalysts. They were to prove themselves highly talented. Their knowledge of our naval cryptosystems dated back to the pre-war years, first to the period of Italy's conquest of Abyssinia, when ships of the Royal Navy patrolled the Mediterranean in support of the sanctions imposed upon Italy by the League of Nations, and then to the Spanish Civil War, when our ships patrolled the coasts of Spain to enforce the embargo of the import of arms. During those years the Germans had ample opportunity to become acquainted with our naval ciphers and codes. An understanding of them indicated the sort of particulars or format likely to be found in later systems – encoded characteristics used when signalling to flag ships, the places in signals where identities of addressees and originators were likely to be found, and so on. The identity of ships under the command of a particular flag ship could often be found from newspapers. Such particulars helped to act as tin-openers to later systems. How many signals our ships exchanged during those years we do not know, but it must have run into many hundreds. Thirty years afterwards an officer could still remember that 7761 meant new paragraph and 4834 a full stop;[28] where particulars of a code become so ingrained in the memory, it is clear that it should have been changed long before it was. What was overlooked was that even the most harmless signal might give away the missing clue for which cryptanalysts had been searching and that any system that remains in use so long is likely to be read by others from whom it is intended to be kept secret. Over-confidence in the security of systems is a common problem. At all events, well before the first U-boats took up their waiting positions in the Atlantic, B-Dienst had had ample time to acquaint themselves with the cryptosystems of the Royal Navy and to read regularly the signals intercepted by them. One historian states that as early as 1936 the Germans were reading the signals of British ships at sea and that this failure in naval security was not overcome until the middle of 1943.[29]   A problem which can arise with naval cryptosystems is that one which is workable in a comfortable office ashore, undisturbed by what is going on outside, may be difficult to use on a vessel which is rolling heavily in an Atlantic gale. This point arose when America was brought into the war and the need for a common system was discussed with the Admiralty.[30] The Americans thought that the one suggested would present difficulties to junior officers operating at sea.* Systems that were not reasonably simple to operate also involved delay.

A second difficulty could arise from putting too much work onto the radio operator. Coded call signs were intended

---

* An example of what could result from mistakes occurred at the Battle of Cape Matapan in March 1941, when a corrupt cipher unfortunately delayed a Greek destroyer flotilla which arrived too late for the engagement, though in time to rescue 100 Italians.[31]

only for those to whom they were addressed, but if a commanding officer wanted to keep himself fully informed about what was going on, he imposed on his radio officer a heavy burden. Code signs were changed frequently; "degarbling" corruptly encoded signals became something of an art and not one which was enjoyed.[32]

We are given to understand that about ten days before the outbreak of war, certain unspecified precautions were taken by Naval Intelligence.[33] But their effect of interrupting the reading of signals must have been fairly modest, for the enemy were soon reading those concerning the North Sea where some of our submarines were deployed. When in November 1939 the *Rawalpindi* was sunk by the *Scharnhorst* and *Gneisenau*, B-Dienst were reading our signals concerned with counter-measures; and they knew that Loch Ewe was being used as a base for the Home Fleet, something that the Admiralty treated as a closely guarded secret.[34] Indeed the enemy had managed to lay mines in Loch Ewe five weeks before 4th December when the *Nelson* struck one and was damaged.[35]

At this stage the U-boats were not using group tactics but were operating singly, and radio discipline was excellent in marked contrast to what developed later. Routes, meeting points and so on, contained in instructions from headquarters, all had encoded identifications, and all a U-boat commander had to do was to acknowledge advice and indicate with a single letter his choice of alternatives.[36] In the early months of the war British cryptanalysts were unable to read the signals that passed between Doenitz and his U-boats, partly because of the nature of the system and partly because of the small number of intercepts and their brevity. It is not therefore so surprising that many vessels were being used to search the seas with the result that a convoy might be left with only a single escort ship.[37] For it was certainly later than April 1940 that effective readings were made of Enigma signals[38] used throughout the German Navy and in particular by Doenitz and his U-boat commanders.[39]

* * * *

In the first few months of the war the U-boats (still very

few) showed reluctance to engage convoys when there were other targets, and by the end of 1939 they had sunk only four ships in convoy.[40] But unescorted vessels suffered considerably more severely from attack, and mines were a menace.[41] The number of U-boats then operating at any one time was usually nine. Two were also maintained on weather patrol and this was continued throughout almost the whole war.[42]

Fierce gales in the autumn and also in the early months of the winter brought some respite, though ships sailing in ballast had a rough and often hazardous time, shuddering and rolling in the heavy seas. These conditions did not help the U-boats either, for though B-Dienst were reading our signals, these could not be put to maximum effect. Whereas in September the tonnage of merchant ships lost was 153,879 and in October 134,807, it fell in November to 51,589 and in December was 80,881. The total losses in 1939 of 421,156 tons represented 114 merchant ships.[43]*

Losses of ships in convoy rose sharply in February, amounting to forty-five vessels totalling 169,566 tons; numbers of escort ships were detached from their convoys to sweep the seas in a vain search for the enemy.

For the Royal Navy also 1940 began badly. Three of their submarines were lost in the Heligoland Bight. The Admiralty wisely and immediately ordered a drastic cut in the ciphers to be carried on submarines, and these were to be different from those used by surface warships.[44]

German records indicate that the Admiralty made partial changes in their codes on 22nd March 1940 and again on 22nd April, but these probably represented little more than nuisance value, for B-Dienst recorded that they must allow but ten days to a fortnight during which their monitoring service would be unable to read signals.[45] It is clear that B-Dienst were well aware of plans for operations in Norwegian waters before early April, when they took place. For on 15th March they advised that the British submarine deployment in the North Sea off Skagerrak and the Heligoland Bight was being dispersed, and they concluded that in consequence of the unexpected Finnish peace with

---

* Unless otherwise stated, figures for losses refer only to those from U-boat attacks.

Russia, planned operations against Norway had been post-poned.[46] They partially decoded an order from the Admiralty to the Commander in Chief, Home Fleet, regarding Plan III from which it was evident that preparations for embarkation of troops on a major scale were by then complete. To top it off, they intercepted a report of the Finnish Minister in Paris of an indiscretion by the French Prime Minister, Paul Reynaud, which provided warning of the British plan to mine certain Norwegian waters.[47]

From the strategic importance of Narvik as a port through which supplies of Swedish iron ore would pass when the ice had gone, the enemy might well have expected us to give it our attention in the spring. Similarly we might equally well have expected that they would know that. In fact the British intention had apparently been known to them since early in October[48] and, according to Schellenberg, Hitler's decision to occupy Denmark and Norway resulted from his knowledge of British plans[49] reinforced by other evidence; thus, the Abwehr reported that the Chasseurs Alpins were being withdrawn from the Metz sector of the Western Front.[50] Accordingly the enemy were not taken by surprise when on 15th April an Anglo-French force landed near Narvik, followed by a further landing of French troops on 20th. Kept fully briefed about Allied intentions, the enemy were able to plan and practise a deception which, as Churchill later admitted, completely outwitted us. On 2nd May the Allied withdrawal began.

No doubt it is always easy for a later generation to look back and criticize those who did not have the foresight to anticipate what subsequently came to be recognized. But it does nonetheless seem strange that our tactical signals were given *en clair*. Evidently it did not occur to those concerned that they might be giving anything away. Thus the Commanding Officer signalled to his team at one stage: "I am steering for the entrance of Narvik Harbour." He was then only a mile and a half away from an enemy warship.[51] So the Commodore of the German squadron had some helpful and interesting information at his disposal. In fact it might not have helped much if the signal had been encoded, for it might still have been read. As one naval author has

remarked, the Royal Navy would certainly have been ap-
palled had they realized the insecurity of what they considered to be their high-grade systems in the hands of the
brilliant intelligence organization of the enemy.[52] This is no
doubt so, but tactical codes must be read quickly if they are
to be of use and, writing of events of 1941, another naval
historian records that they were rarely read in time to
provide advance information.[53] It is evident that the need for
them was learnt from experience in the Norwegian cam-
paign. But the enemy's cipher-breaking service remained
extraordinarily successful; that it continued to do so well for
so long was due no doubt mainly to misplaced confidence at
the Admiralty in the standard of their ciphers,[54] mistakenly
regarded as high-grade.

By the time this ill-fated expedition set sail from Rosyth
on 10th April, it had had one effect helpful to us. Hitler had
ordered Raeder to move all his U-boats from the Atlantic to
Norwegian waters; subsequently the number was reduced to
a score, but even that must have been unwelcome to Raeder
who was accustomed to putting first things first. This was by
no means the only time Hitler eased the strain on Britain of
the Battle of the Atlantic.

It was some time before the Norwegian expedition set sail
that British cryptanalysts had penetrated the secrets of the
Enigma machine, but it was probably not before about May
1941 – possibly earlier – that they had settled down to
regularly reading large numbers of the enemy's naval signals,[55] he fruits of what was to be known as the Ultra
Secret.* The administrative arrangements (Special Liaison
Units in the field) provided for the needs of the Army and
the RAF, but the Admiralty had to make other
arrangements for their ships at sea and transmitted information in their own systems.[57]

The revelations of Ultra, it has been fairly claimed, were
the hub of the Battle of the Atlantic[58] and enabled Naval
Intelligence to read many of the instructions and much of

---

* While one speaks of the Enigma cipher, there was really a number of
ciphers from the Enigma machine, used for various purposes, often
simultaneously; at least thirteen were known to us by code names but
not all were read.[56]

the information sent to U-boats and often to learn the positions of the U-boats from the signals they sent back. On account of the exceptional security value of Ultra, officers in command of ships at sea could not all be privy to the secret and, if on occasion they decided to extend their hunt for U-boats, that was something that had to be accepted. If the Admiralty signals did not result in the U-boats being found and attacked, they nonetheless often enabled escort commanders to alter course if need be. By keeping convoys posted as they did, the Admiralty inevitably ran the risk that the enemy would deduce that we were reading their signals, but it was one which had to be taken, for if we had lost the Battle of the Atlantic, we should have lost the war. Looking back, we must conclude that, in balancing security against needs, the First Sea Lord judged it nicely.

Though most of the Admiralty's valuable information came from reading enemy signals, on occasion helpful advice was received from other sources; thus, the British agent at Riga, until the Russians moved in, was able to keep Naval Intelligence posted with the strength and dispositions of most of the German Fleet at Hamburg and in the Baltic.[59]

At the end of the first twelve months twenty-eight U-boats had been sunk; the enemy had constructed as many new ones, so that his strength was no more than it had been when war broke out.[60]

Though certain changes had been made in our cryptographic systems before August 1940,[61] they do not seem to have troubled B-Dienst very much. But it appears that on 22nd August Naval Intelligence made simultaneous changes in all their codes and ciphers, both administrative and operational.[62] B-Dienst were therefore back to square one. According to German records the Admiralty had maintained the same systems since before the war; the conclusion must be that such changes as had been made were relatively minor or at least not basic and to have caused B-Dienst no more than short-lived inconvenience. A major change had been expected by the enemy long before.[63]

The enemy certainly had some good fortune with armed raiders, particularly the *Atlantis* which on 11th July 1940 boarded the *City of Baghdad* and seized the Merchant Navy code book before the captain could throw it overboard.* This code was known as BAMS (Broadcasting for Allied Merchant Ships). On 10th September the same raider secured papers, including secret mail, from the *Benarty,* but a bigger haul was obtained when they boarded the *Automedon* on 11th November and secured fifteen bags of mail, including no less than a hundredweight of decoding tables, fleet orders, gunnery instructions and intelligence reports. These last named had been drawn up by the Planning Division of the War Cabinet and contained thè latest appreciation of the military strength of the Empire in the Far East with details of deployment and equipment of RAF units and of naval strength, and assessments of the roles of Australia and New Zealand, and even a long paragraph about the possibility of Japan entering the war, together with copious notes of the fortifications of Singapore.[64] The *Atlantis* captain must have been pleasantly surprised to find that the *Automedon* was carrying all that secret mail. It was commonplace for captured papers to provide such information as swept channels, routes, instructions about making contact with other ships at sea, perhaps something about those ships, and even the current code book in use. But this must have been an unusually informative killing. However, the *Atlantis* did not have much longer for these raids, for on 22nd January 1941 the *Devonshire* sighted and sank this raider. By New Year the Admiralty had become aware of the possibilities of these captures of codes and on 3rd January instructed merchant ships to deliver the envelopes containing their code tables to the Naval Control Service Officer at their next port of call.[65]

But if on occasion the enemy struck such a windfall, it is doubtful if B-Dienst often got much from it that they did not know already:[66] the odd "pinch" now and again no doubt, but in the main they were dependent on their own talent and hard work. As Doenitz himself has recorded, his team of cryptanalysts were able, time and again, to provide U-boat Command with just what they wanted to know about British convoys and their whereabouts.[67] B-Dienst were remarkably quick at unravelling new systems. Thus, on 21st August 1940

---

* Code books are bound in lead covers so that they can safely be thrown overboard, should occasion require it.

Operations Room, Fighter Command, where the operations of the German Air Force against Britain were plotted. The first readings of Enigma ciphers were made shortly before the Battle of Britain.

The C-in-C, Western Approaches, in his Operations Room,
showing the plotting of U-boats, first done from reading German
naval signals by about May 1941.

they recorded that changes had been made in all codes and ciphers of the Royal Navy and anticipated about six weeks before they would be reading the new ciphers. By this time the information provided by B-Dienst, based on reading over 2,000 signals a month, amounted to the following: the times of arrivals of convoys at British ports and which ships sailed for which ports (in turn enabling useful conclusions to be formed about convoy time-tables), information about escorts successes and any U-boats sunk, and approach points for ships sailing independently as well as those sailing in convoy, including numbers of independents.[68] Considering all the information B-Dienst was able to provide, it was fortunate that the *Queen Mary* and *Queen Elizabeth* managed to escape trouble. The *Empress of Britain* was lost with all hands.

At this stage, too, radio discipline was well maintained. Though surface vessels of the German Navy evidently did not show the same spirit that they showed in the First World War,[69] the U-boats certainly gave a formidable account of themselves. When it was realized that we were taking regular bearings on even the brief signals that the U-boats trans- mitted,* commanding officers were ordered to use radio only at the beginning of operations or where they were sure that their positions were already known to us.[71] Almost through- out the conflict U-boats proved to be virtually immune from surface or airborne search except when in the proximity of

---

* Bearings were taken by shore-based high-frequency direction-finders (HF/DF) which were developed and refined during the war years. One station would ascertain that a U-boat was somewhere along a certain line of bearing. Others, taken from stations on different parts of the coast would do the same, and the point at which the bearings crossed determined the position. It did not matter for this purpose whether the U-boat signals could be read; the fact that the U-boat was transmitting was enough to fix its position. The margin of error in cross-bearings increased with the distance; for a U-boat in mid-Atlantic an error of ten to fifteen miles was considered very good but it could be much more, depending on how far away the U-boat was. On occasion it produced a bull's eye. Thus on 30th June 1942 a U-boat signalled: "There is nothing to report." Direction-finders at three American stations located it; the U-boat was found with the crew sun-bathing on deck, and that was the end of that U-boat.[70] It was in that same month that escort vessels themselves were fitted with direction-finders and thereafter the exact pin-pointing of U-boat positions became a more frequent oc- currence.

convoys, and sweeping searches for them by escorts were a waste of effort.

Considering the difficulties under which he laboured, Doenitz did extraordinarily well. The Royal Navy had co-operation from RAF Coastal Command, though its effectiveness was slow developing; the figures for U-boats sunk by aircraft mostly refer to the period after the Battle of the Atlantic had been won.[72] Doenitz, however, never had such support or indeed any from the German Air Force. "Everything that flies", said Goering with extravagant gestures, "belongs to me."[73] He would not give the Navy the help requested, though his Focke-Wulf Kondors had a range exceeding that of our own Coastal Command aircraft. He would use them, however, to attack merchant ships and during the opening few weeks of these attacks they sank thirty ships.

However, after the surrender of France in June 1940 Doenitz acquired a notable advantage with our sea communications immediately on his doorstep; in the following months he established a U-boat base at Lorient and made Paris his headquarters.[74] A large number of ships sailing independently, and others sailing in convoys weakly defended were attacked.

Britain's shortage of escort vessels remained a problem, but in September 1940 an agreement was made with America for fifty over-age destroyers in exchange for certain air and naval bases; while these vessels were a welcome stop-gap, they could do no more than cushion the shock of the convoy battles in the Western Approaches. The figures bore out the need for more convoy escorts; thus, from July to October 1940 U-boats sank 144 ships sailing independently and seventy-three sailing in convoy.[75] It was in October that a slow convoy of thirty-four ships with an escort of two old sloops and a single corvette was attacked by eight U-boats; in three successive nights twenty of the ships were sunk,[76] an ominous indication of what was lying in store as regular practice.

*　　*　　*　　*

The year 1941 opened with advantages to both sides but more particularly to the Germans. British vessels used against the U-boats were fitted with radar; at that time it was not rotatable,[77] but was soon to be developed. Against that, B-Dienst were reading signals to the Commander in Chief, Western Approaches, and the Merchant Shipping code introduced in the New Year was soon prey to the skill of Doenitz's cryptographic staff and by 17th March we were in trouble again.[78] Traffic using it had of course increased considerably; its call sign was distinctive, enabling it to be picked out,[79] and Doenitz called it the Convoy Code. Both sides were by now reading each other's signals, neither at the time aware of it. Losses of merchant shipping were mounting and it was fortunate that U-boats were still so few.[80] In January Hitler in one of his erratic bursts ordered a substantial concentration of U-boats to the Mediterranean; at first it was twenty-five, raised to thirty, and by then there was only a small number left in the Atlantic. Losses incurred by this deployment had to be replaced and temporarily the pressure on convoys was eased.

Though America had not then entered the war, B-Dienst noted that they had abandoned the simple code they had been using and on 4th April brought into use a much more complex one.[81]

When the strength of the U-boats in the Atlantic had been restored and then increased, convoys found for the first time a regular and more formidable type of attack than hitherto, that of wolf-pack formation. Hitherto operations had been carried out mostly by U-boats singly, but now they began assembling in groups, advised of our convoy movements ascertained by B-Dienst. Strung out in mid-Atlantic, they awaited convoys by day. As soon as a U-boat sighted one, beacon signals would be sent to others and the convoy would be shadowed, U-boats closing in after dark when, in wolf-pack formation the attack was made. Escorts were often outnumbered by U-boats,[82] though Doenitz found that twenty U-boats in a pack were about the maximum that could be controlled round a convoy without confusion or risk of collision. Losses of merchant ships inevitably rose. The U-boat menace was further worsened when what were known as "milch cows"* were introduced by the enemy in April 1942.[84] These tankers enabled U-boats to re-fuel in mid-Ocean and considerably increased the number of U-boats in operation at any one time. The nature of these milch cows came to light in an unexpected way; an illustrated brochure, circulating in Scandinavia, provided a photograph of one.[85]

It was not difficult for instructions to be sent, moving U-boats into the anticipated route of the convoys, for their course was known together with the number of ships, sailing date, speed and destination, all obtained from reading signals. Unfortunately in September 1941 further changes in the system, designed to make signals safer, seem to have made them easier to read.[86] Sometimes instead of the shadowing reports from the U-boats, U-boat Command received fresh intercepts showing that convoys had made changes of course. This happened several times. Such evasions must have demonstrated that we were remarkably well informed about U-boat dispositions. Fortunately the conclusion drawn by the enemy was not that we were reading his Enigma signals, as of course was the case; instead the spectre of treachery was raised.[87]

Though there were successes – the capture of a U-boat complete with cipher in May was one; another was captured in August[88]† – the menace of B-Dienst remained. For what Doenitz called our Convoy Code was not his only source of information. Another was a signalling system linking service posts with the three Government Offices, Foreign, Dominions and Colonial, also read by B-Dienst. It was used by consular offices for reporting shipping movements from neutral ports; it also included information about ships sailing independently and on occasion measures taken against the menace of armed raiders. By July 1941 it was suspected that these

---

* Milch cows were large submarine tankers, specially constructed to provide U-boats with oil, spare parts, food, clothing, torpedoes, fresh water, medical supplies and equipment, and even replacement crews.[83]

† It was of course the rule to keep secret the capture of a U-boat, lest the cipher be changed. An occasion when this was overlooked occurred in July 1943 when the Italian submarine *Bronzo* surrendered and Eisenhower mentioned it to two newspaper reporters who of course published it.[89] However, Italy was by then a spent force.

signals were being read and another system was introduced.[90]

By this time, however, Hitler ordered that attacks must be confined to ships identified as hostile on account of the appearance of the American battleship *Texas;* in effect this considerably diminished night attacks for a time.[91]

However, on 11th December 1941 Germany and Italy declared war on America and shortly afterwards U-boats were sent to American waters to attack shipping in harbours. What became known to the enemy as "the American shooting season", begun in January 1942, was costly to our Allies. There being no black-out, targets were silhouetted against city lights, tankers and the larger freighters being picked out for preferential treatment.[92] Within six months the enemy estimated that they had sunk some 400 ships with a total tonnage of about 2,000,000. Losses of tankers in the Gulf of Mexico were heavy enough to require that some of our hard pressed escorts be diverted there.

The enemy continued to use the Enigma cipher, unaware that since the spring of 1941 his signals had been read. Minor changes were made every day and at longer intervals major ones. Unfortunately, it was one of these changes that defeated Naval Intelligence in March 1942,[93] when we already had enough trouble on our hands. To illustrate the sort of problem, let us consider the game of chess in which each side has 16 pieces, one move at a time, each restricted, yet no two games are identical or, if they are, it must be extremely rare. The permutations and combinations of Enigma were far greater than moves possible in chess.

The unfortunate fact was that the period during which we were reading the signals to and from U-boat Command had come to an end. The U-boats now had it all their own way. Despite losses, their numbers had more than doubled during 1942.[94] Patrol lines could be narrowed to as little as fifteen or twenty miles apart and the chances of a convoy slipping through unnoticed were virtually nil. On occasion U-boats would pursue a convoy, renewing the attack on each of as many as eight consecutive nights over a period of 1,000 miles, and break off, leaving the survivors to finish their course, in order to set about another convoy, sailing in the opposite direction.[95]

Inevitably losses rose alarmingly. In the first seven months of 1942 the enemy sank no fewer than 589 ships in the Atlantic and Arctic waters.[96] In June alone losses amounted to over 700,000 tons, and by the end of the year 1,160 ships totalling 6,266,215 tons had been sunk.[97] By that time stocks of bunker fuel in this country were down to 300,000 tons, no more than two and a half months' supply.[98] In November the tonnage sunk reached the highest figure for any month of the war, 729,160; of the 119 ships lost no fewer than 70 were sailing independently.*

During this phase Britain was also faced with the problem of relieving besieged Malta which had endured 2,470 air attacks. German agents in the Bay of Algeciras had no trouble noting the movements of convoys.[101] Fuel stocks were at danger point and by June 1942, when Lord Gort was made Governor, starvation and surrender looked to be only days away.[102] The Italians' reconnaissance was highly efficient and so was their dive-bombing, far more efficient than that of the Germans in the opinion of Admiral Cunningham who noted that they had full knowledge of our movements.[103] They may have been reading our signals before the Battle of Cape Matapan; we in turn had secured one of theirs through an agent (see page 137).

In addition there were our convoys to Russia, begun in September 1941 and sailing to Murmansk and Archangel. It had been recognized that losses might be heavy, but it was thought worth doing if it helped to prevent the collapse of Russia. There were mixed views about these convoys: General Alan Brooke was against them.[104] But there was a fear at that time that Stalin might make a separate peace with Germany, as Lenin had done in 1917. There was also the idea that, if the Western Allies supported Russia, Communist hostility to this country would cease and that after the war Russia would become a friend of the West. As we were to learn, these views were ill founded, but at the time they seemed reasonable.[105] The old military maxim, dating

---

* Of all ships lost at sea by enemy action during the war 72 per cent were sailing independently.[99] Of all the ships sunk only nineteen were lost when both air and surface escorts were present.[100]

from the Napoleonic wars, "Never march on Moscow", was apparently not heeded. In the event, as Vice-Admiral Schofield observed, there was a complete absence of team spirit shown by our Allies and at Murmansk not even one crane capable of lifting a tank.[106] The fortunes of convoys varied considerably.* Convoy PQ 17 to Murmansk suffered heavily, twenty-three out of thirty-six ships being lost.[109] The enemy knew all about these convoy movements and where to post U-boats, as a Soviet agent in Germany discovered from the Abwehr.[110] It is not recorded that the Russians passed this advice to us; had they done so, the code would certainly have been changed.

Inability to read the Enigma system used by Doenitz and his U-boat commanders, coupled with the vulnerability of the Admiralty's ciphers, could not therefore have come at a time when Britain was more over stretched, and it extended into 1943.

It is not surprising that it was during this period that losses were so calamitous. Thus, on 16th-19th March, two convoys, HX 229 and SC 122 which were at sea simultaneously were both attacked; U-boats numbered forty and in all twenty-one ships (141,000 tons) were lost at a cost to the enemy of one U-boat. How fully informed the enemy were is clear from the fact that up to the opening of this attack U-boat Command were reading sixteen signals[111] to these convoys. During March 108 ships were sunk, a total tonnage of 627,377; and of this number forty-one were sunk in the first ten days. At the end of the year, some months after the

---

* In a statement in the House of Commons on 16th April 1946 the Prime Minister announced that the United Kingdom had shipped 5,128 tanks, 7,411 aircraft, 4,932 anti-tank guns and much other equipment, some of it from Canada, and that lease-lend reports from Washington showed 14,795 aircraft, 7,537 tanks and much other equipment to have been shipped. But sometimes losses were disheartening. Whereas PQ 9, 10 and 11 all got through unscathed, the figures for PQ 17 showed 896 vehicles delivered but 3,350 lost, 164 tanks delivered but 430 lost and 87 aircraft delivered but 210 lost.[107] The total value of military supplies shipped was £308,000,000 with £120,000,000 worth of raw materials, foodstuffs, industrial plant, medical supplies, etc. Over and above this British people contributed £5,260,000 for medical supplies and clothing under "Aid for Russia" charity schemes, while the British Government made a further grant of £2,500,000.[108] Supplies delivered to Russia across Persia far exceeded those sent by convoy to Arctic ports.

struggle had been decided, the Admiralty looked back at the
cost and recorded that "the Germans never came so near to
disrupting communications between the New World and the
Old as in the first ten days of March 1943".[112] At no other
period during the whole war did Britain come so perilously
close to defeat.

We are told that Enigma signals were read by the cipher
service advising the Army and the RAF during the time
when naval Enigma was not being read. Thus in North
Africa the signals were known to Auchinleck in July 1942
and also at the time of Torch, the Allied landing in North
West Africa in November of the same year.[113] Why,
therefore, were the Enigma signals used by the German Navy
not also being read at the same time? It is known that during
1940-42 Enigma signals generally were subject to frequent
changes and that major variations produced problems for
those in charge of the bronze goddess. What happened was
that changes in naval Enigma were not identical with those
used for military purposes. It is known that on occasion
U-boat Command did introduce changes of their own. Thus,
when it became known to them that the *Atlantis* had been
sunk while refuelling, it raised in the enemy's mind: did the
warship *Devonshire* which sank her arrive there and then just
by chance? The same doubt arose when the *Python,* another
armed raider, was likewise sunk. We are told by a former
officer on Doenitz's staff that a special new cipher was then
introduced whereby all references to grid square positions
were to be super-enciphered.[114] What was later more
challenging was that changes to the Enigma machine itself*
were introduced by Doenitz. Yet the brilliance of our cryptanalysts enabled them to break it in a matter of days.[116]

What is curious is that Doenitz observed that U-boat
Command received not only Admiralty signals and instructions for the routing of convoys, but also in January and
February 1943 their U-boat situation reports, which were
transmitted to commanders of convoys at sea and gave pre-

* The Enigma machine was constructed to take three wheels, though there
  were five to choose from; it was not itself enlarged to take more than
  three at a time except when Doenitz temporarily introduced that
  complication.[115] The wheels, each bearing the twenty-six letters of the
  alphabet, were operated by electrical impulses.

sumed distribution of U-boats in the different areas. These situation reports, Doenitz tells us, were of the greatest value in his efforts to determine how the enemy was able to find out these positions. They were no doubt reasonably accurate, because he considered whether his own signals could have been read which in January was not the case and probably also in February. Was the Admiralty's Tracking Room, like Nelson, blind only in one eye? At all events the conclusion which Doenitz reached was that, except in one or two doubtful cases, British conclusions were based on data available from other sources combined with a feasible process of logical deductions, and he mentions in particular airborne radar which enabled convoys to take evasive action.[117]

Certainly Doenitz had excellent reasons to be pleased with the service he was receiving from B-Dienst. Particulars of the various British ciphers and codes used have not been published but one is now general knowledge. This was akin to the one-time random pad except for one vital particular; it was not one time, being in the form, not of a tear-off pad, but of a book the pages of which were used repeatedly. The pages contained columns of random numerals. The sender would include in his signal the page number, column number and number of the line in that column at which the message started; thus, page 17, column 4, line 22 would be represented by 17422. If the first group of numerals at that place in the keybook read 74326, those figures were added to the basic ones for the opening word of the text. We learn that over a period the enemy were able to build up a "shadow" key of their own.[118] The text would normally begin with the identity of whom the signal was addressed to, for example the Commander in Chief, Western Approaches. As the basic cipher groups were known to them, all B-Dienst had to do was to subtract those groups from the corresponding ones shown in the signal and fill in the result in their own "shadow" key. As there were thousands of these signals,* B-Dienst knew the form they were likely to take, for

* It may be that the Admiralty were unaware of the volume of these signals. After the war they learnt to their surprise that at one stage the enemy reported that they had been reading 1,500 signals a month or about fifty a day. It is not clear how many of our signals were read in time to be of operational use at sea.[119]

it was inevitable that a standardized format would develop, so that they knew where to find the starting point to the key, and so on; and when they had got a proportion of these numeral groups established, they were on their way. The remainder followed. Just how long this particular system was used and how long it took B-Dienst to work out enough to read most of the signals we can only surmise; but it appears that the system was in use for about two years, and from the comment of a naval historian it seems that most of this system had been reconstructed by February 1942.[120]

In addition to those of our own signals which up to this stage B-Dienst had unravelled, they are credited with having solved every American one.[121]

However, not all Allied systems became general reading matter to the enemy. For occasions such as Torch new systems gave B-Dienst virtually no chance to read them in time to be of use.[122] Hitler's anger at the surprise of this huge Allied expedition resulted in another order for U-boats to be transferred from the Atlantic to the Mediterranean.

By this time Raeder who had been troubled by Hitler's disruptions of naval strategy, decided that he had had enough. He was then sixty-seven and in indifferent health. Goering had carried on a vendetta directed at him, Hitler had stormed at him, and on 30th January 1943 he resigned.[123] He was succeeded by Doenitz.

As Grand Admiral of the Fleet, Doenitz had a good enough start. German naval warfare had for some time been very largely carried on by the U-boats. There had been no attempt of note to use surface vessels in the Atlantic after the loss of the *Bismarck* in May 1941, but he then had 300 U-boats in the Atlantic, notwithstanding temporary switching to the Mediterranean. In that year U-boats sank 463 ships, totalling 2,586,905 tons, much the greater part of it during the first five months and most of it in the North Atlantic.[124]

But in the spring of 1943 fortunes changed suddenly and decisively. It is not certain exactly when we were again reading naval Enigma but, if the clue came from one of our agents (see page 140), it was probably not later than March. (A cipher key that has defied unravelment for a year could almost certainly have been broken only with some kind of new aid.) In addition the fatal system which we ourselves had been using and had been read by B-Dienst since February 1942 was dropped. In effect Roskill dates this as May,[125] but McLachlan says firmly that it was done in June.[126] The effect of the combination of these changes was dramatic. The convoy SC 130 which arrived at its destination on 25th May was the last one to be seriously threatened.[127]

In contrast to earlier practice, economy in U-boat signals had by now disappeared. It may have been necessary for Doenitz to communicate as often as he did in order to maintain the close tactical control over operations which he wished to do, but signals were now being read. Moreover, direction-finders were playing an increased part; and the task of hunting down U-boats as soon as they gave away their positions was well in hand. Understandably U-boat commanders were no longer keen to make rendezvous with milch cows; for on a suspiciously large number of occasions, it was noted, RAF Coastal Command aircraft appeared just when the pipe-line was stretched between the two vessels and neither was able to dive. The time when in mid-Atlantic one milch cow had refuelled twenty-seven U-boats within five days[128] had gone for good.

By June the picture had completely changed. The transformation was remarkable. Losses of ships in convoy quickly dwindled and in the last two months of the year 1943 no fewer than seventy-two ocean-going convoys, totalling 2,218 ships, reached their destinations without losing a single vessel.[129] May of that year was a black month for U-boats, about a third of them being lost. Their menace could not, however, be ignored, for as late as January 1945 they were still carrying on the battle, operating in the Irish Sea where they sank five ships and damaged two more.[130] But well before then the writing was on the wall. As Doenitz's staff woefully complained, "The enemy holds all the trump cards. They know all our secrets and we know none of theirs", a telling comment on the vital need of superiority in systems. In the procurement and dissemination of information the tables had been completely turned.[131]

In surface warfare it was much the same story as in sub-marine. B-Dienst read nothing signalled to the Home Fleet during the operations which led to the sinking of the *Scharnhorst* off Norway in December 1943. Similarly they intercepted 158 signals at the time of the Anzio landing in January 1944, but made nothing of them;[132] and in the summer of that year a new system used on convoy work likewise defied efforts to unravel it. There was also a Typex cipher used by the RAF, chiefly in the Mediterranean and Middle East which was never read.[133]

The long night was over. But a terrible price had been paid for allowing our defences and the standard of our ciphers to deteriorate during the years when Britain slept.

Once we had really got on top of the job, however, the U-boat menace was killed. A U-boat had only to signal once, however briefly, to be hunted down with the aid of direction-finders. In eleven months nearly 300 of them were sent to the bottom.* For them the lights were already red in May, when forty-one of them failed to return.[135] On 22nd of that month Doenitz in effect conceded defeat by withdraw-ing his U-boats from the Atlantic,[136] leaving only the two weather reporters.

In the same month the German Army was finally defeated in Tunis and the war in the North African theatre was over. Italy was tottering and Mussolini's downfall only a few weeks away. In Russia, von Paulus had surrendered at Stalingrad by the beginning of February and the Russians had got the measure of their foes. These were notable ad-vances to the ultimate victory of the Allies. This was indeed a year of achievements, that in the Atlantic being the es-sential one for Britain and the longest drawn out of them all, because that tense struggle had begun on the first day of the war.

The downfall of the enemy in the Atlantic had several causes, including certain technical and scientific inventions and secret weapons, centimetric radar and high-frequency direction-finders being the dominant ones; the contribution of America, which was of course of immense importance and

* Germany began the war with 57 U-boats and afterwards commissioned a further 1,113.[134] Total losses in all waters were 785.

on a scale which others could not match, though the Royal Canadian Air Force provided valuable help throughout and, so far as circumstances allowed, so did the South African Air Force; the major contribution of RAF Coastal Command followed the appointment of Sir John Slessor as Commanding Officer in Chief in February 1943. Between 1st June and 31st December 1943 a total of 141 U-boats were sunk, 93 of them by aircraft.[137]

We cannot say that all the contributions came from the Allies, for the official historian of the war at sea has this to say:[138]

If Goering's megalomania contributed nothing else to the defeat of his country, his long and stubborn refusal to co-operate with the German Navy, and his recurrent strife with Raeder must have contributed a good deal towards the Allied victory in the Atlantic.

Add to this Hitler's ignorance of naval matters and such influence as Goering was able to exert upon him, and the Germans' contribution to their own defeat is seen in perspective.

It is surely beyond dispute that the unravelling of ciphers and codes exercised a strong influence. If B-Dienst had not been able for so long to read the Admiralty's signals, we would not have faced the perils that we did; when success in reading signals lay wholly on one side and failure wholly on the other, merchant shipping losses rose on such a scale that they could not have been borne much longer. A few months perhaps? Who can say? In no other theatre of war did forces thousands of times as strong as B-Dienst bring us so close to defeat.

The view that in general our intelligence services were superior to those of the enemy is undoubtedly correct. But Vice-Admiral Gretton has commented on the major part played in the battle of ciphers and codes in the Atlantic, concluding with the following passage:[139]

My belief, however, is that in general and especially during the vital spring of 1943, the Germans had the superiority which brought them considerable advantage.

That is one judgement. We know the record of B-Dienst
and of their industry and talent. The story of our own team,
however, has never been told; we know only a limited
amount about it. But we should not forget that in the
construction of cryptosystems – just as important as unravelling them – the systems we used in the second half of
the war did finally defeat even B-Dienst. Perhaps, therefore,
we should leave it at that, so far as we are in a position to
pass judgement. We could, I think, fairly sum it up, as the
Duke of Wellington did after the defeat of Napoleon at
Waterloo: "It was a damn close-run thing."

THREE

THE SECRET SAPPERS
Russian Espionage and Ciphers

Until the Revolution of 1917 Russian governments did not, so far as is known, maintain a much larger body of overseas agents than did other countries; they had no reason to do so, not being concerned to overthrow existing régimes and replace them with their own. They had, however, for a long time employed a secret police force within their own frontiers. It is not, therefore, surprising to learn that the total number of persons charged by Germany with spying for Russia in the First World War was the same as that of those charged with spying for Britain – fifty-five.[1] It is believed that at the beginning of that war Germany had twenty-two agents in this country.* These figures are indicative of the sort of scale of espionage agents then used.

* All but one became known to the police during a visit to this country by the Kaiser in 1910, when his retinue included his Chief of Intelligence, Wilhelm Steinhauer. One evening when the Royal party were attending some function, a detective noticed that Steinhauer left them and took a growler. He was followed and in full evening dress was a conspicuous figure when he alighted in the Caledonian Road and walked to a man's hair-dressing saloon run by one, Carl Ernst. On hearing this, Kell, the head of MO5 (later MI5) – in fact he was its solitary member – persuaded the head of the Post Office to allow mail from this establishment to be opened, such places sometimes being used as secret postal forwarding offices. (There was, and still is, nothing illegal in the opening of mail, though as a common practice is was stopped in 1844.) As suspected, the mail was addressed to Germany and was clearly from agents whose names and addresses were noted. The agents were not arrested at the end of the Royal visit; MI5 has never had powers of arrest and no doubt there were reasons for the course taken. Immediately war was declared, twenty agents were arrested; one, Carl Hans Lody, was not apprehended till October.[2] Years after the war another agent, Jules Silber, wrote a book called *The Invisible Weapon* in which he disclosed that he had worked in the Censor's Office throughout the war, sending his mail to boxes in neutral countries, stamped "Examined by Censor".

It became quite a different matter after the Communists had taken over. In peace time one might perhaps expect the number of agents to subside; it does not follow. We are told that the United States did not have a single espionage agent in Japan in 1940.[3] In marked contrast the total number of espionage cases reported in the *New York Times* between 1917 and 1939 was no fewer than 1,902, Russia being "aggressively involved" in more than 1,500 of them;[4] and that leaves out of account agents who did not come before the courts.

During the years between the wars the Russian espionage system was reorganized. Towards the end of 1935 the existing circuit in Germany was abandoned; probably one reason was that Hitler had come to power and the Gestapo made it necessary to revise the espionage system. A second and dominating influence, however, was Stalin's big purge of 1938 when about 80 per cent of senior Army officers were executed,* and simultaneously nearly all the key espionage agents in Western Europe were recalled and shot.[6] Hundreds of what one authority refers to as "the Communist espionage aristocracy"[7] were included in the general butchery. Early in 1938 Beria was instructed to reorganize the Secret Police, and he set up a number of spy schools. Most of the new men came from the Signals Service, emphasis being on cipher work, and General Peresypkin was appointed director.[8] Training courses at first lasted no more than a few months, the threat of war requiring urgency, so that the great majority of those who were in post when war broke out were newcomers with little or no experience. In Western Europe Belgium was picked for headquarters; the law of treason there was relatively lenient provided that the offence was not directed against Belgium herself.[9]

A number of reports have been published from time to time about what are loosely referred to as the Russian spy schools, and though it is taking things out of chronological order, it is convenient at this point to look ahead at what we understand of their development, because it leads us to the subject of the cipher systems which come into our story and also the scale of Russian espionage.

* On 12th June 1938 Marshal Tchukachevsky and seven generals were arrested and later executed. Hundreds of other arrests followed.[5]

A convoy assembling at sunset, a time-consuming operation, usually known to the Germans during the first half of the war when they were reading Admiralty ciphers.

An ammunition ship exploding on a convoy to Murmansk; the heaviest losses were sustained by convoy PQ17 when, with the Germans reading Admiralty signals, twenty-three out of thirty-six ships were sunk.

It would certainly be surprising if in a tightly-controlled police state nothing was done in the way of preparing agents. Although different countries have different ideas and sometimes they do not seem to bother too much,* any training must be undertaken somewhere. There is nothing secret about where CIA agents are trained in America, that information having appeared in publications some years ago.[11] Russian attempts to throw cold water over the idea that they would do such a thing are singularly unconvincing. They state that they have no spy school in the Ukraine, as they claim the Western World alleges, and invite visitors to satisfy themselves that there is none. That may well be so. (The Ukrainians are traditionally by no means the staunchest supporters of Moscow anyway and indeed are believed to have supplied the West with innumerable agents.[12]) One well-informed and established authority on secret service matters refers to twenty or thirty such establishments.[13] The Special Radio Section in the Lenin Hills which is disguised as an Institute of Gold Research[14] is perhaps as well known as any.

In recent years more than one book has appeared referring to another establishment known as Gaczyna, situated about a hundred miles south-east of Kuibyshev.

We are told that the Gaczyna organization is divided into sections, so that those who are to be active in the United Kingdom are trained at one, those who are to go to the United States at another, and so on. It covers in all some 425 square miles. Each section comprises a model of life in the country concerned, complete with the same type of buildings, shops, clothing, cinemas, hotels and so on, even to selling the same beer, and trainees must speak only the language of that country and accustom themselves to using

* L. A. Nicholson, Britain's agent in the Baltic States before the war and until 1940, when the Russians moved in, was appointed during the Thirties. In his book he tells us something of his experiences, and records that he was left by the Foreign Office to construct his own cipher, although he relates that he was no cryptographer. He was not given advice about how to spy or how to make contacts, but the conclusion he reaches after his own experience leaves a clear impression that he doubts if a general training course was really practicable.[10] Much depends on the functions of the agent and, perhaps even more, the type of person recruited.

the same currency.[15] In effect those who are sent to England live in a model of an English township and learn English ways, even to the game of cricket. American diplomats in Moscow have heard persistent reports of imitation American villages complete with American cars, hamburgers, ice cream sodas and so on.[16]

Some of the German agents sent to this country in the last war made elementary mistakes which immediately gave them away. One of them, just landed in Suffolk, made his way to the nearest railway station and asked at the booking office for a ticket to London. Told that the fare was "ten and six", he put down ten one pound notes and six shillings. On another occasion an agent, asked at the booking office if he wanted a single ticket, replied *"Ja"*.[17] Another agent tried to pay for a meal at a restaurant with a ration card and yet another tried to get a drink at a public house at 9 a.m.[18] The Russian course is designed to guard against such elementary blunders which no doubt it does, though during the war the Russians at times made glaring mistakes. On one occasion they recruited as an agent a German prisoner of war named Heinrich Melchior; his equipment included distinctive Russian boots, map and so on, and some tins of American food bearing Russian labels.[19]

What is surprising about the Gaczyna course of training, which was first started in 1939, is that it is said to last ten years. By that time those coming to this country must have become thoroughly anglicized; maybe, if they talk in their sleep, they do so in English. Whether it is really necessary to take training to such lengths is a matter of opinion. Sir Percy Sillitoe, a former head of the Directorate of Security (in war time MI5) expressed the view that it was a waste of time, manpower and money.[20] During their training, students attend a course at the Lenin Technical School at Verkovnoye. The scale of recruitment into the service can perhaps be judged from the number of students of whom, we learn, 3,072 passed their final examinations in 1970.[21]

The total number of agents employed in the Russian espionage service is of course unknown and estimates vary. Ronald Seth, a SOE agent who was posted to the Baltic States, stated in a book published in 1961 that "it is estimated by experts who have reliable sources of information that non-Russian agents run to between 750,000 and 1,000,000; the backbone of Soviet espionage is, however, the 12,000 Russian nationals".[22] These figures are considerably more than those contained in an unusual report issued by the State Department, Washington, in June 1960; they estimated the total number of "operatives" employed by the Communist nations at about 300,000.[23] (It is not clear exactly what that term covers.) The same report said that some 18,300 people had been arrested in West Germany as Soviet spies since 1952. Other countries in the grip of Communist domination have certainly developed their own armies of agents; in the mid-1950s East Germany was believed to have considerably more in proportion to the total population than the Soviet Union.[24]

Bernard Hutton who at one time worked for the Czech Communist Party and spent four years training in Russia before, being disillusioned, he fled, thought a figure of 250,000 an under-estimate of the total strength of Russia's spy network.[25] The American, Ladislas Farago, said that he would be inclined to put the number of Russia's espionage agents at 250,000 to 400,000.[26] Whatever the true figure, one must assume that it has increased since those estimates were made. Even two years before the publication of that book Vladimir Petrov, the cipher clerk at the Russian Embassy at Canberra, was ordered by Moscow to return, because, it is believed, he was suspected of being involved in the Beria conspiracy to seize power. Defecting, he handed over to the Federal authorities the names of about three hundred agents and potential agents in Australia[27] the total population of which was at that time about the same as that of Greater London.

To put figures in proportion, let us look at the known number of enemy agents posted to this country in the last war. Farago who obtained access to the complete Abwehr records in Washington tells us that his count of German agents in the British Isles during those years totalled 253 and that "the fate of German spies active in England during the Second World War can be cleared up conclusively once and for all. They were either caught, interned and executed, or they were turned into double agents – *all of them*".* He adds that well over 100 became controlled, that is turned into double agents working for Britain.[28] Sir John Masterman, then at MI5, states that his office had personal files dealing with about 120 double agents,[29] the money supplied by the Germans to maintain the system between 1940 and 1945 being something in the neighbourhood of £85,000.[30] A large number of agents were caught almost immediately or soon after their arrival. For, as Masterman remarks, in time of war espionage is difficult and highly dangerous and counter-espionage comparatively easy, whereas in peace time it is the other way about.[31]

On all counts, therefore, Russia has a far larger espionage force than any other country in the Western World. According to Hutton it is well over ten times as large as the combined estimated services of countries in the Western World[32] and, if we adopt the figures quoted by Seth, about forty times as large. There is, however, one major difference in the job, and numbers do not mean everything. The business of a British agent is to obtain information and to transmit it to his superiors; he is not there as a sort of secret sapper to help undermine the regime of the country to which he is posted and replace it with that of Britain. The same cannot be said of the activities of Communists, whether they be paid agents employed by the KGB or active pursuivants and fellow travellers who pass on any information *gratis* or otherwise push the cause. Together they are the creeping horror of the Western democracies. Thus in March 1976 Mr George Young, a former deputy-director of our SIS, stated that a highly placed traitor had penetrated Whitehall or Westminster during the Heath administration, and on the following day he said, "There are three Ministers of the Crown whose formal allegiance to Communism is never known to have been renounced," and he went on to refer to the difficulties others in the government had, keeping secret papers from them.[33] There were then no Members of Parliament who, when elected, stood as Communists.

When we come to consider the unravelment of ciphers in

* Von Schiellermann whose information led to the sinking of the *Royal Oak* was, strictly speaking, a resident British subject. See note on page 149.

the Second World War, it must be taken into account that the Russians use a variety of methods of obtaining information, some of which could lead direct to the keys of ciphers. Thus, in 1945 the Russians presented Mr Averell Harriman, then the American Ambassador in Moscow, with a carved replica of the United States Great Seal. No doubt the gift was accepted with pleasure and warm thanks. The thanks would not have been so warm, had it then been known, as was discovered later, that the replica had a hollowed out cavity containing a vibrator to sound waves of conversations. Likewise, when in 1953 the United States Embassy was moved into premises in Tchaikovsky Street to which three additional storeys had been added, the thick interior walls were later found to contain a network of wires connected with forty microphones.[34]

It is probably the opinion of the majority of cryptographers that in the construction of ciphers the Russians are about as good as anybody. The majority of their cryptosystems are particularly difficult to break and one of them, developed originally by the Germans, is impossible to break. But when it comes to passing judgement on the standard of Russian cryptanalysis, we cannot arrive at a conclusion, for we have no way of knowing how they come by their information. Anyone who has listened in to the clear text of something to be enciphered is automatically provided with at least part of the key to the cipher. To many systems some kind of tin-opener can be found; copies of others are obtained complete by microphotography. Blackmail is also used, as the Vassall case showed. Its use was not confined to the Russians, for in Germany Heydrich had his "Salon Kitty" to which those susceptible to erotic entertainment were invited, the morning after being blackmail day; the Japanese Ambassador was one who was lured there. Considering the alternative, the "turning" of agents could perhaps also be argued to amount to blackmail, though it must be said that the German agents who were turned were not noticeably crippled by scruples. With their various sophisticated devices, some of them introduced into foreign embassies and legations, the Russians have more means at their disposal than other powers.

The story of the Russian espionage network and their secret communications will be better appreciated if we first acquaint ourselves with the type of cipher in which the Russians specialized for that purpose.

The training course for agents includes cryptography. One system, we are told, is established as a basic introduction to ciphers[35] and is certainly simple enough for beginners. It is known by the name of Kiel. A book is chosen and the page for starting the message is stated. If, for example, it is page twenty-three, the first line on that page is brought into use. Each letter, punctuation mark and space is counted and the number of the first relevant letter is written. Only one letter in each line is used. If the wanted letter is not found in a line, the numeral zero is entered. Words are separated by commas between numerals. The method is easy to follow but laborious, and it is not suitable for a long message. The system is, however, noteworthy for one particular reason, that it undermines the basic method of unravelling or breaking ciphers. It was the Arabs who discovered in the fourteenth century the constancy of letter frequencies. In all alphabetic languages certain letters appear more frequently than others, and the same applies to words. As long ago as the sixteenth century stratagems for hiding letter frequencies were established practice in Italy; in fact their effect was too limited to have more than a delaying effect, often rather minor. Higher algebra assists the breaking of polyalphabetic ciphers, complex though they may be. The Kiel system obliterates letter frequencies, because there is no particular pattern, due to the use of random numerals.

During the years between the wars many Russian signals were intercepted by the Americans and efforts were made to read them. Some of them passed between Moscow and an espionage group, ostensibly a trade mission called Amtorg; thousands of these signals were handed over for solution but, though much time was spent on them, none could be unravelled. The reason for the supremacy of Russian cryptograms is largely that, with such a huge espionage service, the one-time key can be plentifully used. It can of course also be used between an ambassador and his Foreign Office. But it cannot be used where what are termed "horizontal" communications arise, because the one-time element is then not practicable, for example between a score of military units any one of which may want to communicate with any of the others, necessitating all having the same key. Apart from that difficulty, the volume of field ciphers in the Second World War was so enormous that all the printing firms in America, producing nothing else, could not have printed enough keys, nor could all the ships in the American Mercantile Marine have carried them. But for espionage work the one-time random pad is ideal.

The traditional Nihilist system embodied the essential of the one-time random pad in that it used random numerals to obliterate letter frequencies. It was simple to use, as the following example shows:

We first construct a checkerboard of the alphabet. Using the Roman one, it is shown below:

	1	2	3	4	5
1	A	B	C	D	E
2	F	G	H	I/J	K
3	L	M	N	O	P
4	Q	R	S	T	U
5	V	W	X	Y	Z

To encipher the word "attack", we pair the numerals and then add a key word used only for this particular message, let us say "lion". The result is as follows:

"Attack"	11	44	44	11	13	25
"Lion"	31	24	34	33	31	24
Enciphered text	42	68	78	44	44	49

Pairing could be done the other way; the letter L, for example, then becomes 13 instead of 31 and O becomes 43 instead of 34. (During the Second World War, Otto Punter, whom we shall come to when we review the network in Switzerland, did it this way.) There were other variants. A key word could be inserted into the checkerboard itself, throwing out of reckoning the normal alphabetic order of the letters.

Modern Russian Secret Service signals are translated into

English before encipherment so that, in the unlikely event of one of them being read by another power, the association with Moscow will not become immediately evident. It is known that 60 per cent of English text consists of eight letters which can readily be remembered in the phrase "A sin to er(r)". We can now see how use is made of this. The example given below represents the type of cipher used in the last war by the Russian espionage service.

We first choose a key word, let us say "Soviet", in which no letter occurs twice. We set out the checkerboard with the key word forming the top line, the remaining letters following underneath. We attach the numerals 0 to 7 to the eight different letters in "a sin to er(r)" as they occur vertically. Thus, as the letter S occurs first, it is numbered 0, while the letter N is the last of these eight letters to occur and is therefore numbered 7. We complete the numbering by attaching two-digit numerals from 80 to 99 to the remaining letters. The following shows this checkerboard as used by Klausen in Tokyo except that the keyword he used was "subway".[36]

S	O	V	I	E	T
0	2	87	4	5	6
A	B	C	D	F	G
1	83	88	91	95	98
H	J	K	L	M	N
80	84	89	92	96	7
P	Q	R	U	W	X
81	85	3	93	97	99
Y	Z		/		
82	86	90	94		

We can reproduce this in a different form of checkerboard as follows:

	0	1	2	3	4	5	6	7	8	9
	S	A	O	R	I	E	T	N		
8	H	P	Y	B	J	Q	Z	V	C	K
9		D	L	U	/	F	M	W	G	X

We now set forth the plain text of our message, entering

the equivalent numerals underneath. Thus the word "documents" is enciphered as follows:

D	O	C	U	M	E	N	T	S
91	2	88	93	96	5	7	6	0

If numerals occur in the plain text, instead of spelling them out we use oblique strokes on either side to show that the numerals between them are plain text and are not enciphered. But we enter each numeral twice. Thus "80" is represented as follows:

9 4 8 8 0 0 9 4

The completed numeral text is finally set out in groups of five; if necessary the addition of 0 is used to make up the final five.

To the completed enciphered text of the message itself we now add numerals which have nothing to do with the text but are introduced so that the result is a jumbled lot of numerals. The numerals we add are usually taken from a book. If it is ordinary text, the selected passage is enciphered in the same way as the text of the message itself. If it is statistical, the figures are added in direct. Addition is what is called "modular", that is there is no carrying forward. Thus, though 5 and 7 make 12, the 2 is entered but the 1 is disregarded.

Last of all, an indicator group must be provided so that the recipient knows where to find the key passage in the book. Suppose it is on page 127, line 4 and the second word (or column 2, if it is from a statistical list); this becomes 12742. For security's sake this is disguised, for example by adding it to the third group of the text. The result is then entered first. The recipient subtracts what has become the fourth group in the signal from the first (indicator) group and hence obtains the key.

This cipher can be varied, no two agents within the same network using identical systems. For example, in the original checkerboard the keyword, itself variable, can be placed in the second line. Likewise, there can be the addition of superencipherment, entailing adding on another layer of enciphered material, and even the form of this can be varied, for example by omitting every other numeral. Similarly in the indicator group the numerals can be put in rearranged order, lines can be measured from the bottom of the page and words from the end of the line. Various combinations of these and other adaptations suggest themselves. It does not matter what form these detailed differences take, so long as the recipient knows.

We conclude by making the acquaintance of the one-time random pad to which brief reference has already been made. It was developed by the Germans after the First World War[37] and the Russians, with their quickly expanding espionage service adopted it as ideal for that purpose. Each leaf of the pad which may be no larger than a book of postage stamps and, as used by the Russians, was smaller, consists of random numerals written in groups of five in columns. On half the pages the numerals are printed in black; these are used by the agent for his outgoing signals. On the other half they appear in red and are used by headquarters for their signals.

The agent memorizes a word or phrase from which he soon learns his checkerboard; ignoring the first group of numerals on the leaf of his pad, used as an indicator, he then adds his enciphered text to the numerals on the leaf in use. As soon as he has completed his signal, he destroys that leaf; and when the recipient has deciphered the message, he does the same. Thus that particular table of random figures no longer exists. If the recipient afterwards wants the message confirmed, the agent in replying must use another leaf.

Because this cipher involves random numerals and each key is used once only, it is unbreakable. The only dis-advantage is that, if a suspect is caught in possession of a pad, there can be no doubt about his activities, whereas if he uses a novel or other book which might be found in any house, no suspicion is aroused. The risk with the book system is, on the other hand, that if the enemy should ascertain the identity of the book, he may be able to break the cipher, so long as he can ascertain the right page, line and starting word in the same edition of the book.

The fact that these systems are known does not weaken their security, for the one-time random pad is perfectly safe and, so far as the other system is concerned, the number of books published in this country in a year runs into thousands, and there are innumerable old ones, not to mention all the books in other languages in which the twenty-six-letter Roman alphabet is used; and numbers of these have appeared in more than one edition. Icelandic books could not be used, as their alphabet comprises thirty-three letters, and the same applies to Danish with a twenty-nine-letter alphabet. But Italian with twenty-two letters and Romanian with twenty-three could be used. (In practice the remaining letters of the twenty-six letter alphabet are known to both those languages, occurring in a few foreign words used and in foreign names.)

FOUR

LE GRAND CHEF
Leopold Trepper and the Rote Kapelle

At the time when war broke out, Russia had an extensive network but during the early phases of the conflict it was by no means a going concern in some countries in Europe, mainly reflecting the results of the big purge in 1938. Whereas the butchery of senior army officers (down to the rank of colonel) may have demonstrated Stalin's determination to eradicate any rival persons or groups which might develop, the purge of men in the espionage service was probably due to well-founded suspicions that years spent in lands of freedom were contaminating. The complete reorganization of the secret services, however, also involved newcomers at headquarters, including the cryptographic service, and this no doubt accounted for the shortcomings and indeed the extraordinary inefficiency that provided the backcloth against which the drama of the Rote Kapelle was played. At the headquarters in Moscow – usually known as the Centre – some remarkable blunders were made. Indeed the Director himself had taken a course in ciphers, but evidently not in security of which he must have been remarkably ignorant. He did not seem to be aware of the development of direction-finders in which Russia herself was quickly in the field, possibly even ahead of Germany, and of the consequent dangers of transmissions from fixed points over fixed hours, or of the risks involved in a network in which practically everyone knew everyone else, or even of the hazards of a signal containing the addresses of senior officers in the service. So inefficient were they that some of their men within the Swiss network, to which we shall be coming, including the principal operator, wondered if their contact could really be the Centre.[1] These results of what in vulgar English would be called a "crash course" – evidently more crash than course – were to cost the Russians dear.

Before the Germans launched their attack on Poland on 1st September 1939 Russia's two leading agents in Germany, Harro Schulze-Boysen and Arvid Harnack, had got together in Berlin, but time was needed to build up contacts, for one blunder in choosing these could bring about the undermining of the whole network. We learn that Alexander Erdberg, the Soviet recruiting agent in Berlin – also known as Karl Kaufmann – had meetings with his two senior agents on 14th June, 1941, and that two groups were formed, Schulze-Boysen's and Harnack's. This was only eight days before Germany launched her attack on Russia. It appears that they received their assignments, radio equipment, ciphers and such training as they had undergone, not more than a month or two earlier, and that they were still groping their way towards a proper professional standard.[2] During that period Harnack managed to transmit a few signals to Moscow, but they had not got into their stride by the time the German attack was launched.

The network quickly began the process of infiltrating selected quarters which included the Abwehr, the German High Command and virtually every government ministry. In addition, besides Berlin there were agents in Vienna, Madrid, Oslo and Zurich; Schellenberg mentions, too, Copenhagen, Stockholm, Budapest, Belgrade, Athens, Istanbul, Rome, Barcelona and Marseilles.[3] They had their fingers in plenty of pies.

That part of the network which principally operated in Germany, Belgium, Holland and France was called by the Germans Rote Kapelle (Red Orchestra) for the Russian called a short-wave wireless set a music box[4] and the man who operated it a musician or conductor. The outstanding figure was Leopold Trepper who was not accorded an orchestral position but was known as *Le grand chef.* Had the Centre been as efficient in their administration of the system as he was in leading it, the period when it enjoyed maximum success would certainly have been longer and might conceivably have survived the whole war in good shape. They made cardinal blunders and the remarkable thing is that Trepper survived. He owed it entirely to his personality, for he never put a foot wrong.

In the story that follows we shall confine ourselves to the principal characters. There were many others, and a comprehensive record of their activities makes a sizeable study.

Trepper was a Polish Jew, born on 23rd February 1904. In his youth he developed strong Communist leanings and during the Pilsudski régime he spent some months in prison. He was released without trial. He afterwards joined Hechalutz,[5] a Zionist body which was financed by wealthy American Jews, and in 1928 he went to Palestine where under the name of Leiba Dab[6] he obtained employment, first as a member of a gang of road workers, then on a kibbutz, and finally as an apprentice to an electrical engineering works.

Probably in or about 1930 Trepper managed to enter France illegally, staying initially at Marseilles, and it was in that country that his career as a Soviet espionage agent had its origin.

Trepper was an interesting character with a taste for fine paintings, books with old bindings, and good food and clothes; he was also one of the many admirers of Edith Piaff.[7] He married a girl, Maya, who was four years younger than he was but had already been married and divorced. He had first met her when he was in Palestine where she had fled, being then wanted for "political murder".[8] She, however, does not come into the story that follows. After it was all over Trepper rejoined her and settled in Poland, not having seen her, so far as is known, for at least fifteen years.

Moving to Paris after his arrival in France, Trepper made himself known at the Soviet Embassy where he evidently impressed them, and he was sent to Russia to be trained.

Early in March 1939 he took up his appointment in Brussels. He then had a Canadian passport. There his two assistants were Leo Grossvogel and Hillel Katz, both Jews and the latter Polish. Grossvogel was a merchant trading in rainwear and soon a cover company was developed with branches principally in the Low Countries and in France, but also in Scandinavia. Posing as a French Canadian, Trepper travelled frequently from his house in the Avenue Slegers in Brussels to Paris where Anton Danilov was responsible for liaison between the Soviet Embassy and the network in Belgium and Holland.

Two other agents who joined Trepper and were to play more prominent parts than Grossvogel or Katz were Michail Makarov and Captain Victor Gurevich-Sukulov (or Sukulov-Gurevich). Makarov was believed to be a nephew of Molotov, then Soviet Foreign Minister, and probably was. Both affected to come from Uruguay. Makarov's alias was Carlos Alamo and Sukulov had a passport in the name of Vincent Sierra, though he preferred his code name of Kent. Both these men had served with the International Brigade during the Spanish Civil War; Makarov had been an air pilot. In accordance with Moscow's policy Trepper developed an espionage group in Paris where he was joined by one, Henry Robinson (one of many aliases), who came from Frankfurt and in August 1940 introduced links with the Vichy Government.

Sukulov was a senior member of the Russian network; he had been instructed by Moscow to establish a circuit of agents in Copenhagen for infiltration into Germany. He had been concerned with that part of the espionage network that operated within Germany itself where one of the principal characters was Arvid Harnack. In Berlin government circles, Harnack was regarded as a brilliant economist and was employed at the Ministry of Economics, being responsible for the allocation of raw materials. His code name was Caro. He was the son of an eminent theologian. His wife was an American Jewess. Another whom we should note at this stage was Harro Schulze-Boysen who worked for no less an organization than Forschungsamt, Goering's Air Force secret service instrument which collected news of all kinds from all quarters and, in particular, specialized in breaking and reading enciphered signals. Goering made use of the Enigma cipher – very frequent use, too. Certainly, Schulze-Boysen was rightly regarded as a man of moment; he did not lack daring and, so far as it was relevant, he moved in the cream of Berlin society.

There were others. One, less conspicuous than Schulze-Boysen, was Adam Kuckov, a journalist and writer employed by a publishing firm. Others employed in influential positions at various ministries included Franz Schelche, First Secretary at the Foreign Office, and Rudolph von Schelhia, also at that office and another of the senior aides of von Ribbentrop who, like all the senior Government Ministers, had his own cipher specialists. Not only that, but von Schelhia's apartments became a favourite meeting place in the evenings for the whole diplomatic colony.[9] There were also the Countess Erika von Brockdorff at the Ministry of Labour and Horst Heilmann, at one time at Goebbels' Ministry of Propaganda and subsequently employed in the Air Force Signals Service, and there were numerous others in less prominent positions. The man who mattered most was Schulze-Boysen. Though the division of responsibilities left him in charge of collecting information and Harnack responsible for its transmission, Schulze-Boysen was the more dominant character.

At its peak the group is believed to have numbered more than a hundred leaders and hundreds of regular agents and informants.[10] Transmission was not up to standard, however, Hans Coppi, the chief operator, being inefficient. They do not seem to have conducted themselves with much circumspection, for most of them knew everybody of importance in the network. But they evidently exercised a degree of independence. The Centre may have wanted transmissions regularly at fixed hours according to a schedule, but Schulze-Boysen was informed about German developments of direction-finders and knew better than to make himself and his associates sitting ducks. He was aware that aircraft fitted with direction-finders sometimes circled overhead and that vans, similarly equipped, were often on the prowl; and he then went off the air.[11] Transmitters had to be unpacked and assembled for each operation and dismantled, packed into a case and removed afterwards; and sites had to be carefully chosen. Hotels were no use, for when the transmitter was plugged in, others' lights would have dipped. But vacant places offered opportunity – a doctor's surgery, a dentist's, shop and business premises, a school or even, we are told, the back room of a beer garden on occasion.[12]

There is no doubt that Trepper and his associates who were based in Brussels were genuine Communists, though like most Communists, their principles faded obligingly when opportunity enabled them to acquire wealth and property. But it is a reasonable question whether the team based in Berlin were quite such staunch supporters of the faith. Were they not principally members of the anti-Hitler underground? But for the Nazi régime, would they have thrown in their hands with the Russian espionage service? It may be so, but there is room for doubt at least about some of them. Harnack was evidently well regarded in Moscow and one, Greta Lorke, said that he was on the Soviet books in 1933, the year when the Nazi régime was established.[13] One may well have doubts about Schulze-Boysen. Certainly he organized the network and was principally responsible for making it a going concern. We cannot be sure of the answer to this question, but at times Schulze-Boysen showed a marked degree of independence which was certainly not the way the Centre wanted it. It is perhaps a fair conclusion that they were a genuine part of the Russian network, chiefly because the Nazi régime was hateful to them and stimulated their wish to help Russia to bring about its downfall, and that the independence of the Centre's orders which was demonstrated by their irregular transmissions stemmed from the independent character of Schulze-Boysen himself.

We shall be returning later to this section of the network.

In their personalities the agents who operated in Brussels differed considerably. Trepper was the ideal type for that particular job, what the Americans call "a natural". He knew all about Winnipeg, his alleged place of origin, and could talk with an apparently intimate knowledge of life there; his French was excellent and he also spoke German fluently. At no time did his vigilance relax, unlike that of his fellow agent, Sorge in Japan, who left enough secret papers about to hang him. Trepper made no mistakes. Nor did he lose any opportunity that presented itself; highly intelligent and completely under control, he was an excellent head of the network. He was accorded by Moscow the rank of a Red Army general.

Makarov, however, was not so well suited to the job. He was inclined to be showy, rather than inconspicuous, and he liked fast women and fast cars. Fast women did not matter much and, considering the life agents led, never sure that the next day would not be their last, who can blame them? But fast cars did matter, since they attracted the attention of the police, particularly if there were accidents.[14]

Sukulov was apparently a vain man; however, he was not only an accomplished linguist but, when in a difficult situation, he evidently kept his head well.[15]

Trepper's team in the office where transmitting was done was joined by two women. One of them was Sophie Posnanska who went under the name of Anna Verlinden and had originally made the acquaintance of her chief in Palestine. She was certainly not lacking in character or in courage either, as she was to prove. She did the enciphering of the signals for Makarov to transmit. The other was a woman named Rita Arnould, a German Jewish emigré, not long widowed. She was house-keeper and on occasion acted as courier. Whereas Posnanska was undoubtedly a willing and determined agent, on the evidence Rita Arnould was not and probably never wanted to get involved in espionage work. She was, however, in financial straits and accepted the job.

Trepper was able initially to send information to Moscow via the Soviet Military Attaché in Brussels. But the task was a time-consuming one; moreover, once Germany turned her attention to the west, Belgium would soon be overrun. (Brussels fell on 17th May 1940.) Moscow ordered that the team were to transmit direct and to do so regularly every night from midnight to five a.m. This prize blunder is hard to credit, when we remember that in mid-June 1940 the Russians, having occupied the Baltic States, were themselves using direction-finders to locate illicit transmitting stations.[16]

After Canada had come into the war, Trepper could no longer conveniently pose as a Canadian businessman, and he was provided with a fresh passport in the name of Jean Gilbert. He developed his circuit in Paris where he came into contact with French aristocracy and also Russian emigrés. When opportunity served, he used these occasions to establish further links; thus he met one Baron Vassili Maximovich, the son of a former Czarist general, who maintained a liaison with Anna-Margaret Hoffman-Scholz who was a secretary in the German Consulate. Trepper set up a business in Paris under the name of Simex. He was often to be seen in the company of German officers who happily stood him drinks and chatted to him, unaware that their companion was the head of this sector of the Russian espionage network.

Sukulov meantime formed what he called the *Société Importation-Exportation* (Simexco). The office was at 192 Rue Royale. He must have chuckled to himself when the Abwehr innocently issued passes to senior Simexco employees and even consulted them about building projects.

In the earlier phases all went well. Trepper obtained the information. Sophie Posnanska, on the ground floor, enciphered it and Makarov, on the floor above, transmitted it night after night between the prescribed hours with the call sign PTX. In addition, Moscow received irregularly what the Schulze-Boysen team had to tell them. Not only that, but part of the network operating from Switzerland also kept them supplied; the story of this sector will be told separately. The air was full of these transmissions which were incomprehensible to the Germans who in the earlier stages did not know where they came from or who was conveying them.

The value of Trepper's information was certainly evident to Moscow in June 1941, for more than once he had given warning in advance of the attack which the Germans were to launch on Russia. The final one was given early on Saturday, 21st June, when Trepper asked Major-General Susloparov, Military Attaché at the Vichy Embassy, to convey the warning of the imminence of the attack. Stalin did not believe it, though Trepper was far from the only one to give him that advice.* Subsequently details of the German High

---

* The Germans were aware that Stalin had been warned, for a top secret communication from the German Foreign Office to the German Ambassador in Moscow on 22nd April 1941 reported the contents of a warning given by Sir Stafford Cripps, the British Ambassador in Moscow, and stated that it had been delivered on 17th April.[17] As a result of Stalin's refusal to pay heed to these warnings, on the first day alone 1,811 Russian aircraft were destroyed, 1,489 of them on the ground; and in the first four weeks the Germans advanced 400 miles.[18]

Command's strategic plans, including the offensive on the river Dnieper, together with the date, were transmitted to Moscow.

Neither the Funk-Abwehr (counter-espionage specialists in radio transmissions) nor the Gestapo can have had any illusions about the existence of a Russian espionage network. The number of signals which had been intercepted quickly ran into hundreds. It was but a question of time before tracking devices for locating transmitting stations were brought into play, and it was only a matter of months after Hitler had launched his attack on Russia when they were used to hunt down the source of the transmissions. At first it was thought to be on the Baltic coast, possibly in the neighbourhood of Danzig; as the Russians had moved into Lithuania, as well as Latvia and Estonia, on 15th June 1940, this made sense. An intelligence unit was operating in the Russian consulate at Danzig up to the time of the German invasion of Russia.[19] It had two functions; one was to recruit agents, both Germans and Poles, and the other was to transmit to Moscow. But this unit was not the one sought. The problem led to discussions between General Thiele, Chief of Wireless Security, Admiral Canaris, head of the Abwehr, Schellenberg who was answerable to Heydrich, and Heinrich Muller of the Gestapo.[20] When a number of direction-finders got to work, they were not long getting onto the real source. Three long-range direction-finders, one at Breslau, a second at Oslo and a third at Brest, all took bearings. At such a range the location could be ascertained only approximately, but they pointed to somewhere on or near the coast of Belgium.

Franz Fortner, the Abwehr man in Ghent, was told to make investigations but he drew a blank.[21] Narrowing down the search first to Bruges and then to Brussels, German Intelligence instructed their senior man in Belgium, Captain Harry Piepe, to find the transmitting station. It was commonplace for espionage units to be camouflaged as merchant companies and sometimes counter-espionage would do the same. On this occasion Piepe set himself up as a Dutch businessman of the name of Riepert and established himself in the rue Royale. By an extraordinary coincidence he took premises at number 192, the address of Sukulov's Simexco company. In fact they were not only on the same floor but adjoining, being separated at one point by nothing more than a glass door. However, it was not this that led to the exposure of the transmitting station in the rue des Atrébates, neither company having any idea at the time of the true *raison d'être* of the other.

Towards the end of November, five months after the attack on Russia had been launched, Piepe secured the latest type of close-range direction-finding equipment and detector vans which of course kept in touch with one another, coasting about the streets of Brussels, their listening interfered with here and there by electric railway lines or high tension wires. Efforts were first concentrated on the various districts and use was made of the ruse which became commonplace, of briefly switching off the electricity supply to a district or sub-district during the hours of transmission; when transmission stopped immediately, they knew that they were getting close to their quarry. In this way they succeeded in narrowing down the hunt to the Etterbeek district of the city. Once they had established that the site was in the rue des Atrébates, they were near the end of their search. Short-range direction-finders could be conveniently carried under a coat and there were even miniature ones which could be worn in the ear like a deaf-aid. Slowly walking along the street, the response they got was that the origin of the transmissions was number 101.

Soon after two a.m. on the morning of the 13th December Piepe, ten men from the Military Police and a small body of soldiers approached the building, all wearing socks over their boots. One writer comments that Makarov had left no guard outside; in fact at that hour his presence would have made him conspicuous, but it seems that nobody was watching from the windows either. Suddenly Piepe's men burst into the house and raced up the stairs. On the second floor they found the transmitter which was still warm. On the floor above they awoke Rita Arnould who was in bed; she was scared out of her wits. Returning to the ground floor, they found Sophie Posnanska, photographic apparatus, invisible ink, cultures which could be used for creating epidemics,[22] some papers including some charred remains which had evidently been hastily thrown onto the fire but had not burnt properly, but no code book.

The three prisoners were taken away and two policemen were left in charge of the building.

Now occurred an incident which illustrated the thoroughness and the never-failing vigilance and cool nerve of Trepper. About nine o'clock on the following morning he arrived at the house, unaware of what had happened. To his surprise the door was opened by the police who asked him what he wanted. He produced a bag of rabbits and explained that the lady of the house was accustomed to buying them off him and he wondered if she wanted any.* Having no particular reason to doubt his story, the police asked to see his papers; they seemed to be in order and he was told to make himself scarce. He did so and warned others in the network.

This was not the only bit of cool cheek that Trepper and his men got away with, for after the police had been withdrawn a few days later, two men called at the house and calmly removed the books.[25] Since it was general knowledge among cryptographers that the Russians often used books for providing cipher keys, it is surprising that Piepe's men had not already removed them.

It had been suggested that after the closing down of this transmitting station Trepper joined the *Maquis*. It does not seem likely, nor does it fit what is known of the timetable of his movements. He was by training and experience a secret service agent, and guerilla warfare in the mountains would not have been much in his line. He did apparently at a later date consider setting up a centre in North Africa but the Torch landing knocked that on the head. He did, however, agree to Sukulov setting up a centre in Marseilles. He himself made for Paris. Unfortunately the Centre had failed to equip

* This is the version given by Piepe and generally accepted.[23] Interviewed some years after the war and asked if this was correct, Trepper inquired who had related it. When told that it was Fortner, he replied "He would" and gave a different version. This was that he said he had an appointment at a garage nearby and produced his Todt Organization pass.[24] That version clearly does not sound nearly as convincing, as it provides no reason for calling at the house.

the French part of their network with radio transmitters while there was still time, having depended on Brussels as the communications centre. Accordingly Trepper was without direct means of getting in touch with the Centre where no doubt suspicions would have been aroused when the regular nightly signals were no longer forthcoming. It was not apparently till February that Trepper made contact with the French Communist Party and sought their help. They allowed him to use their transmitter, but limited him so much that it was quite inadequate for his purpose. A home-made set was produced; it was too weak to reach Moscow but with it Trepper communicated with the Russian Embassy in London.[26]

The loss to the Russians of the transmitting station in the rue des Atrébates was serious and gave cause for anxiety. Another agent in Brussels, Constantin Yepremov, who posed as a Finnish student, was told to take over, his colleague being a Prussian, Johann Wenzel, who was a wireless specialist known as "the professor". Evidently the Centre were giving Trepper notice. They also tried to strengthen their numbers, a few agents being flown from Murmansk to Manchester, but forbidden of course to converse with their British helpers even about such unoriginal subjects as the weather. They were parachuted into France but were quickly picked up, the effort proving futile.[27]

Yepremov was by no means the equal of Trepper. Moreover, if one transmitting station in Brussels had been hunted down, the probability was that another there would share the same fate. There was, too, the risk that links with other parts of the network would be traced, even that centred in Berlin itself. There was indeed good reason for anxiety in Moscow.

The beginning of the undermining of this network came at a time when the Russians had enough troubles on their hands, without losing such sources of information about the enemy's plans on the field of battle. The inglorious seizure of Finnish territory* to safeguard Leningrad had proved

---

* Finland was attacked on 30th November 1939. The Finnish Army was small with practically no armour, no anti-aircraft guns and an Air Force with only 100 aircraft some of which were unfit for service. The Russian

completely ineffective; in that city about a million people
had died already of cold and hunger in only the first few
months of what was to be the most prolonged and terrible
siege in history.† On the field of battle the Russian armies
were engaged with those of the enemy over a front of almost
1,500 miles. Much ground had been given and prospects
must have looked grim, because it was not long before the
Soviet Government and the Diplomatic Corps moved to
Kuibyshev, though Stalin himself remained in Moscow.
Churchill had thought the odds five to four that Moscow
would fall by October,[32] and indeed by November the German vanguard was only twenty miles from the city. Not
many senior British Staff Officers then thought that Russia
would be able to stand up to Germany for long;‡ the prospects for the summer of 1942, when the enemy's offensive
would be resumed, were indeed worrying, as Molotov
emphasized during visits to London and Washington in
April.[34]

The one overwhelming advantage the Russians had, when
Germany launched her attack, was the widespread espionage
network. With all the information they had been getting
from it, including Forschungsamt's cryptographic records,
particulars of new aircraft (such as the Messerschmidt 210),
various secret weapons, details of monthly productions and
of food and fuel supplies, and the extent of the anti-Nazi
underground movement in Germany, all on top of advance
advice of the enemy's battle plans, together with numbers of
tanks and aircraft, the Russians had found the going hard

---

force was estimated at 1,200,000 men with 1,500 tanks and 3,000
aircraft.[28] Peace was made on 13th March 1940, Finland ceding 25,000
square miles of which the population of 500,000 voted unanimously to
be evacuated.[29] It is related that the Italians were shocked by this attack
on Finland and sent assistance;[30] whatever it amounted to, it was
unavailing. The poor showing of the Russian armies no doubt reflected
the purge of most of the senior officers in 1938.

† When the siege began, the population was over 3,000,000. In January
1942 a resident Russian newspaper correspondent recorded in his diary
that deaths then numbered 6,000 to 8,000 daily. In January 1944 when
it was all over, the population was estimated to number only 560,000.[31]

‡ At that time Field Marshal Sir Alan Brooke had not met Stalin who, he
later said, had the most brilliant military brain and the coolest head of
anyone he had ever met.[33]

enough. The survival of their espionage system meant much
to them.

*   *   *   *

Of the three prisoners two refused to talk, Makarov and
Sophie Posnanska. Makarov survived; his relationship with
Molotov may have saved him, just as the survival of Peter
Churchil of SOE is believed to have been due to his in-
correctly supposed family connection with the Prime
Minister. Makarov was imprisoned, first in Germany and
later in Italy; he was found by the Americans in 1945 and
released. He was lucky. The woman was less fortunate. She
would say nothing and, forestalling execution, she committed
suicide.

The only one who opened out was Rita Arnould. In return
for an undertaking that, if she would tell them all she knew,
her life would be spared, she agreed to do so. To encourage
her, she was accommodated at a hotel for a time but, after
she had fulfilled her part of the bargain, she was beheaded.
Exactly how much she knew and was able to reveal to her
captors may be doubted. But she did give them one most
valuable piece of information that ultimately provided the
key to reading the enciphered signals, and these in turn led
to the exposure of the network in Germany itself.

Among the various papers collected from the rue des
Atrébates was a piece of charred paper lying in the grate. No
doubt efforts had been hurriedly made by Sophie Posnanska
to burn the papers when the police were heard racing up the
stairs to the transmission room. Had this piece been properly
burnt, what Rita Arnould told her captors could never have
been put to such good use and the Berlin network would not
have been dynamited. On this scrap of paper Piepe's men
were able to distinguish part of an encoded working; if they
could ascertain from that the key-word and the source in
which to find it, success should be possible.

At this stage the German Signals Service formed a team
who were sent with instructions to unravel the system. The
senior member of it was a young schoolmaster named
Wilhelm Vauck; he brought with him a group of students,

some of them linguists and the others mathematicians. The extent of the infiltration by the Russian espionage service is shown by the fact that, in addition to the young students, the team included Horst Heilmann, one of Schulz-Boysen's men, used by the Signals Service to read English, French and German signals.

For six weeks Vauck and his team worked away, trying to open up the cipher from their precious piece of paper. The furthest they could get was to reconstruct the single word "Proctor". Given that that was correct, the problem was to discover the source. Who or what was Proctor? At this stage Captain von Wedel arrived. Aware that the traditional Russian system involved the use of a book, he interviewed Rita Arnould and asked her what books Makarov had been reading. She had been housekeeper and must have seen books lying about. What were the titles and who were their authors? She remembered seeing a number of books in the room used by Sophie Posnanska and named them.* Von Wedel sought the books most of which he was in time able to get from second-hand book shops. He read through them industriously day after day, but none of them contained the word "Proctor". There was, however, one book which for some time he was unable to trace. Book publishers could not help him; and it is not surprising that even the *Bibliothèque Nationale* could offer no advice for, in the accepted sense of the word, it had never been published. It was entitled *Le miracle de Professeur Wolmar* and the author was Guy de Téremond. It had been issued by the Paris periodical *Le monde illustré* back in 1910 and had been sent to regular subscribers as a free supplement; on the cover were the words "Not for sale". It takes a devious mind indeed to look back and find such a well concealed source and, if Rita Arnould had not mentioned it, it is most improbable that it would ever have been discovered. After an extensive search von Wedel who had hunted Paris for a copy eventually unearthed one. He was fortunate indeed to do so. Therein he found the long sought "Proctor".

Vauck's team set to work and, though at first it was slow

* Schellenberg tells us that there were eleven books in all[35]; Perrault says that the number recalled by Rita Arnould was five.[36]

going, they were later able to decipher two or three signals a day, and by and by to decipher about a third of the signals of which they had records. One of the more recent ones with a number of its own indicated the considerable number of previous signals. Most of the old signals were dead, so far as their usefulness was concerned, but on 14th July 1942 the diligence of this industrious team was rewarded by one prize. This one of the earlier signals had been sent from Moscow to Kent (Sukulov) and read as follows:

From Director to Kent. Personal. Report immediately Berlin three addresses indicated and determine causes failure radio links. If stoppages occur, undertake transmission personally. Efforts three groups and transmission vitally important. Addresses: Neuwestend, Altenburger, Allee 19, third right, Choro – Charlottenberg, Fredericstrasse 26a, second left, Wolf – Friedeneau, Kaiserstrasse 18, fourth left, Baur. Send Eulenspiegel back here. Password: Director. Report progress by October 20. New (repeat new) plan in force for three stations.

Investigation revealed that "Choro" was Schulze-Boysen, "Wolf" was Dr Adam Kuckov and "Baur" was Arvid Harnack.

This team had been signalling the Centre with secret information. Aircraft and vans equipped with direction-finders had been searching cities for the origin of these signals, hitherto defeated by transmitters going off the air when the hunt was in progress. It was because of this irregularity that the Centre instructed Sukulov to go to Berlin and find out why communications from that source were so often disrupted. He there met the two senior men, Schulze-Boysen and Harnack.

In some 500 reports[37] Schulze-Boysen had provided Moscow with a wide range of information, some of it of considerable value. This included full details of the enemy's plans for the offensive in the Caucasus. When he was told that the Russians had been advised of this, Keitel could not believe it. Whether, as has been claimed, the Rote Kapelle contributed materially to the Russian success at the Battles of Stalingrad in the winter of 1942 and of Kursk in July of the following year, perhaps seems open to question, for before then the major part of the network had been undermined.

Schulze-Boysen was a striking figure, the tall blond Aryan type that Hitler extolled, intellectually exceptionally gifted, even brilliant, and possessed of plenty of independence and of great courage. But we do not get the impression that he could match Trepper for reliability. He seems to have been immature in some ways and liable to be erratic.

The feat of Vauck and his team of unravelling and reading the fatal signal to Sukulov, giving the addresses of the three chief conspirators in Berlin, marked the end of the existing network in Germany. There could not have been a more dangerous signal. It may be that, even if it had not been sent, sooner or later the Germans would have discovered the plotters. But with all the addresses in one signal, they were provided with practically everything they needed to know.

According to Schellenberg, the revelation of the Berlin network was the outcome of joint surveillance between General Thiele, Colonel von Bentivegni of Military Intelligence and himself, and the first culprit discovered was Colonel Becker of the Engineers; he says that subsequently Schulze-Boysen and others were arrested.[38] This, however, is twisting the facts. The fatal signal was revealed three weeks before the surveillance arranged by Schellenberg and his colleagues; and it was that signal that undermined the Berlin network.

On 30th August Schulze-Boysen was arrested as he was leaving his office; his wife was also arrested. Harnack and his wife were spending the day at a seaside resort when they were taken. By the end of the first week after this exposure virtually the whole network had been revealed and a total of 118 arrests made. Sixty-four death sentences were passed; the first were carried out on 22nd December, eight men and three women being executed, including Schulze-Boysen and Harnack and their wives. Schulze-Boysen's courage never failed him. Before his execution he was visited in his cell by his father, on the orders of the Gestapo in a vain effort to get him to talk. The brief account of their last moments together makes poignant reading.[39]

In Moscow the Centre received advice from Rado, the head of the network in Switzerland who in September sent the following signal:

To Director from Pakbo.
In September an extensive organization was uncovered in Berlin which sent messages to the Soviet Union. Many arrests have already been made and others are imminent. Gestapo hopes to expose the whole organization. Head of the organization and wireless operators have been arrested. Exposure was due to radio direction-finding. Dora.

The exposure no doubt came as a shock to General Gehlen, Hitler's Chief of Intelligence in the war against Russia. He would have had even more of a shock if he had then known that the head of his own Russian counter-intelligence service was himself a Russian agent, one Heinz Felfe.[40] However, he had no reason to be squeamish, for sometimes the boot was on the other foot; Gehlen himself is credited with having infiltrated agents into Stalin's War Council and also the headquarters of Marshals Zhukov and Koniev.[41]

*   *   *   *

Being a wanted man, Trepper had to keep on the move in Paris, but he nonetheless showed that his hand had lost none of its cunning. Nor did his ability to winkle out secret information desert him, for, as later transpired, he knew in October 1943, and possibly earlier, about flying bombs and where the launching pads were being built, though the first of these did not fall on London till the following June.* This information might have come to him through his Simex

* A security risk arose with these missiles, for the enemy naturally wanted to know where they had landed and obituary notices might have given the answers away. An evening newspaper, without appreciating this, published a map showing the sites hit. Fortunately, however, this information never reached the enemy. In any case agents in Britain who had been "turned" (see Chapter 7) were sending misleading information. Had the enemy learnt the truth, the rockets which followed in September would no doubt have been better aimed; as it was, they were largely wasted effort. (Though invariably referred to as ten-ton rockets, in fact they exceeded twelve and a half tons.) These missiles destroyed in all 29,400 houses and damaged some 250,000 others.

company which became the main supplier to the Todt Organization, mobilizing for the construction of Hitler's Atlantic Wall, his own Maginot Line and the largest building project of the war. The two companies waxed prosperous, turnover being huge. Trepper purchased a castle in Central France where his agents could stay for a rest, and also a farm. Sukulov in turn moved into a most capacious villa on the Boulevard Whitlock in Brussels; he installed a mistress there and evidently looked after himself in style, having some fifty suits.[42] Moscow might think they had finished with Trepper, but he had other ideas. In fact he succeeded in infiltrating agents into virtually every office of importance in Paris. Nothing succeeds like success, so we are told; and at that stage Trepper might have been headed for the top again. But it did not work out that way.

Early in January 1942 a direction-finding unit was moved to Paris and on 10th June narrowed down their hunt to the suburb of Rueil-Maison. The arrest of a couple, Hersch and Myra Sokol, followed; they were two of Trepper's aides. Almost simultaneously the transmitter worked by Yepremov and Wenzel went on the air and was located at Scharbeek. When the raid was made by the Police, Wenzel who operated the transmitter got away over the roofs, but he was afterwards captured. A number of messages for the Centre were found, still uncoded, giving information about German production of arms, losses and reserves. Wenzel looked a tough customer and evidently his captors treated him that way. Whether he talked or whether it was Yepremov who was not in the building at the time of the raid, it was revealed that Trepper was in Paris where he directed the Simex company. Wenzel later (January 1943) succeeded in making his escape; he knocked out his guard, seized the keys and vanished. However, that is taking us a bit ahead of events.

In the summer of 1942 Piepe and his men were back in Paris where they installed themselves in the rue des Saussaies. By then Trepper who had his ear close to the ground was lying low. He had good reason, for on 12th November Sukulov was arrested. Piepe had discovered that Sukulov was fascinated by a Hungarian girl, Margarete Marcza (code name "Blondine"). She did not betray him but it was correctly anticipated that she would lead them to him.[43] This was not Piepe's only stroke of luck, nor the most remarkable. By chance he discovered Trepper's dentist, a certain Dr Malplete. He went to see him one morning and asked who his patients were and his next appointments to see them. The dentist consulted his engagement book and mentioned, among other things, that Gilbert (Trepper) was due that afternoon at two o'clock. Piepe did not give away which of the patients particularly interested him. What was clear to him was that by sheer luck the visit could not have been better timed. Accordingly on that day, 24th November, while Trepper was seated in the dentist's chair, the police walked in and arrested him. Trepper took it calmly.

The Germans were now working the "play-back" game, that is they sent bogus signals to Moscow as though they had come from their own agents. The probability is that the Centre was taken in by this. The style of those operating radio transmitters is somewhat akin to handwriting. One may have longer pauses than another, there are differences in speed and rhythm, and a listener who knew the style of his contacts could recognize such personal peculiarities. As the Germans had got Wenzel to work the transmitter, the Centre might well have thought the signals genuine.

With Trepper, Sukulov, Wenzel and Yepremov under lock and key, not to mention some of the smaller fry, and with the "play-back" game going strong, it all now looked one-sided.

But Trepper was not the sort of man to lose his nerve. He knew so much that Carl Giering, his principal captor, sought to win his collaboration. If Trepper closed up, or if he were executed forthwith, much valuable information would be lost. Each of them played for time. There were a number of conversations between him and Giering; while we do not know the full story of Hiem, Trepper kept his secrets. He was evidently well treated and was even allowed to move about Paris, though accompanied always by his Gestapo guard, one Willi Berg. But some months later, when no doubt Berg's vigilance was slackening, an incident occurred which gave Trepper his chance. The guard with whom Trepper was then on easy, even friendly, terms became ill one day with

stomach pains. Trepper said he knew of a remedy which
could be bought at Bailly's near the Gare St Lazare. This
firm of pharmacists occupied the whole block, comparable
with that in London between Shaftesbury Avenue and
Coventry Street, facing Piccadilly Circus. There were several
entrances and exits. Trepper got out of the car. To his
surprise Berg, perhaps on account of his illness, perhaps
partly due to over-confidence, did not get out and accom-
pany him. He never saw Trepper again.

Trepper walked into the Gare St Lazare from the rue
d'Amsterdam and boarded a train for St Germain-en-Laye
where Georgie de Winter who had been his mistress lived. He
knew, however, that it would not be safe to remain long with
her, and indeed she was soon afterwards arrested. Ever
vigilant, he remained in hiding until the Allies entered Paris
(25th August 1944). All that time there was a hue and cry for
him, but he was never again caught. Finally, in November
1944 he received word from Moscow that there would shortly
be a seat on an aircraft leaving Paris. On 6th January 1945
he was aboard. The aircraft took a roundabout route with
stops and delays, and it was not till the fourteenth of that
month that he presented himself in Moscow.

Of what happened to the Rote Kapelle it is difficult to be
sure. Schellenberg records that it continued to operate until
the end of the war,[44] and Leverkuehn, head of the Abwehr
in Ankara, gives his opinion that it was never concluded but
continued in the years after the war.[45] Hoehne takes a
different view; he thinks it exaggerated.[46] It may well be that
it was not completely finished, but it seems an inescapable
conclusion that it never fully recovered its earlier successes
after the direction-finders had moved in. The days when an
espionage network could transmit from a fixed address in
enemy occupied territory were already running out fast when
Germany attacked Russia. When things were going well for
the Rote Kapelle, however, it was certainly an efficient unit.

The Centre's insistence on regular transmissions is difficult
to understand, for the development of direction-finders, like
that of radar and other inventions, had made fast progress
and made it virtually a suicidal policy. From their earliest
days SOE warned their agents on no account to transmit

either at regular times or from fixed points. Schulze-Boysen certainly knew better than to do that, and one might have expected the Centre to learn from him.

When Trepper was interviewed in Moscow on his return, the Director's opening question was to ask him what plans he had for the future, a thinly veiled hint to Trepper that he was expected to fade out and keep his mouth shut. But Trepper was not by nature the sort of man to go quietly away and keep his thoughts to himself. Mistakes had been made and it was the Centre who had made them. He had three times given Stalin advance warning of the German attack on Russia in June 1941, and no notice had been taken of it. Moreover, the administration of the network had left much to be desired. Regular transmissions were bloomer number one. They in turn brought about the disastrous signal to Sukulov, giving the addresses of Schulze-Boysen, Harnack and Kuckov. One might have expected them to arrange a rendezvous with Harnack alone, as he was in charge of transmissions; even Kuckov, a comparative beginner at the game, knew immediately from that stupid signal that the worst was likely, as he nervously told his wife.[47] The whole network in Germany was undermined by that blunder, reinforced by another arising from the inadequately instructed team; for it was well established practice that not more than three persons in a network should become acquainted with one another, to avoid the risk of an agent who had been caught and tortured giving away the whole network, a rule that had never been applied to the Berlin network. Moreover, there was the inadequate equipment of the Paris centre. What Trepper said at the interview we do not know. But the blame for this catalogue of elementary errors lay with Moscow; Trepper knew it and Moscow knew that he knew it.

It was clear that Stalin would not stand for having such a man at large. There was only one place for him, the Lubianka; and so this remarkable personality who had served Russia so well was given, as the reward for his services, fifteen years in the Lubianka prison where others, in particular Sukulov and Wenzel, were also serving terms, though Trepper of course was not allowed to meet them.

After Stalin's death (5th March 1953) and with the coming
of Kruschev with his ideas of limited liberalization – which
did not last long – Trepper was released, having served
almost ten years. He afterwards rejoined his wife and settled
in Warsaw.

*   *   *   *

How valuable to the Russians was the information they
received from the Rote Kapelle? It is difficult to be sure. At
one extreme Perrault maintains that no other intelligence
service matched it in keeping the Russians posted with the
enemy's plans[48]; and certainly Professor Dallin who was
rather less given to the use of superlatives also thought highly
of it.[49] At the other extreme Hoehne considered it to be of no
decisive value and that, if it had not existed, the war would
still have taken the course it did.[50] Rowan and Deindorfer
take a middle view, holding that it kept the Centre well
posted with the enemy's plans for the autumn of 1941 and in
particular for operations on the Dnieper; and they hold that
to the end the Rote Kapelle continued to operate and to
provide helpful and welcome intelligence.[51] Paul Schmidt, a
German diplomat, had a high opinion of the Rote Kapelle.
No doubt we can conclude that the Lucy network in Switzerland, which we have yet to consider, was of greater value
still, partly, though not only, because it continued to operate
uninterrupted for considerably longer. But it is perhaps
worth noting that despite the independence they exercised
contrary to the Centre's orders, Schulze-Boysen, Harnack
and Kuckov were all posthumously honoured by Moscow for
transmitting what was described as "much valuable information".

While there were exceptions like Sophie Posnanka who
refused to talk and took her own life, some of the agents in
Trepper's team who were caught did give away information,
excluding Trepper himself, and some probably gave away
practically everything they knew. One may hold the view
that this was deplorable, and so in a way it was. But Moscow's treatment of their agents was totally different from
that of, for example, SOE and their agents. Though of course

mistakes were made there too, there could never have been any question of cruel or unjust treatment or, need one say, of imprisonment or other means of suppressing their right to talk and write afterwards. Both British and French subjects were working for countries that were the homes of freedom and of the Christian faith. There were numbers of them, girls included, who were subjected to torture before execution but gave nothing away, going silently to their deaths. If, on the other hand, they survived, their seniors were of course delighted.

It was not at all that way in Moscow. Whether agents were welcomed or were incarcerated depended not on the services they had rendered, but on what suited the convenience and purposes of the administration. Their agent, Richard Sorge, who was posted to Tokyo where he was eventually caught and hanged, was posthumously showered with honours and recognition, though not till more than twenty years after his execution. There is no adequate explanation of this sudden and unique burst of hero-worship. But no doubt there were reasons for it. Yet the job that Sorge carried out was not extraordinary and was performed in much less difficult or dangerous conditions than those in which the Rote Kapelle operated; indeed conditions could hardly have been less difficult or dangerous for that type of job. For one thing Sorge was not posted to enemy-occupied territory; during the time that he was active, Japan was not at war with Russia* or indeed with America or Britain either. Did the Russians not learn that, when caught, Sorge offered to turn his coat and spy for Japan? If, instead of being caught, he had returned safely to Moscow and had then had criticisms to make of the Centre, would he have been honoured? On the contrary, he would have finished his career in the Lubianka. Russia's agents themselves were mostly pretty tough characters unimpeded by pernickety scruples. They cannot have been so green that they were under illusions or were unaware of the purge of 1938. They knew quite well the sort of people they were working for; is it surprising if that, when they were caught, they looked after themselves?

* Russia declared war on Japan on 8th August 1945, only six days before Japan's surrender.

FIVE

THE MAN WHO KEPT A SECRET
Lucy and the Swiss Network

At Krien near Lucerne there is a tombstone which bears the following brief inscription:

Rudolph Roessler
1897-1958

That is all, and that is how this unusual man would certainly have wanted it, for nobody ever kept a secret better than he did. He died with his secret – how he obtained the most comprehensive and continuous service of intelligence yet known to history – and it is unlikely now that we shall ever be able to do more than hazard a guess.

Roessler is said to have been born at Kaufbeuren in Bavaria, the son of a forester, and is usually accepted as having been a German, though one of his colleagues in the network believed him to have been a Czech.[1] In the First World War Roessler served with the German army and afterwards settled down as editor of the *Augsburger Allgemein*. In 1928 he went to Berlin as secretary general of a body promoting theatre culture. Five years later he chanced to meet Dr Xavier Schnieper, a German Swiss; Hitler had just come to power and Roessler expressed to his acquaintance his dislike of the Nazi régime and his fears for the future. Schnieper suggested that he move to Switzerland. Roessler took his advice and settled in Lucerne with his wife and became director of the Vita Nova publishing house.

We are told that at one stage of his pre-war career Roessler was an agent for the Czechoslovak Secret Service, and also that he returned to it after the war. Both these beliefs seem to be established fact; certainly the first makes sense with what followed during the war when he certainly did not give the impression of being a beginner.

In the early months of 1939 the Swiss General Staff, mindful of the threat of war, looked to their Intelligence Service to keep them posted. The head of it was Lieutenant-Colonel (later Brigadier) Roger Masson who maintained connections with corresponding services elsewhere, in particular those of Britain and France. Under him was Major Waibel who was in charge of the Bureau Rigi which specialized in intelligence about Germany. About April 1939 Schnieper, who lived in Geneva where he had periodically acted as interpreter at the International Labour Exchange, was appointed to a post on Waibel's staff. He was instrumental in introducing two new members. One was Rachel Dubendorfer, a Pole by birth and divorced, and the other was Roessler who was recruited probably in the autumn of 1939.

At some stage, not later than February 1941, the information contributed by Roessler had made such a strong impression that it suggested that he had excellent contacts. Some of these reports were shown to Sandor Rado who had been resident director of the Russian network in Switzerland since 1936 and was one of the few in Western Europe who had escaped the purge. It was in this way that the Russians came to be provided with a phenomenal, continuous intelligence service.

The number of agents is said to have been about fifty.[2] The network operated from four centres, Geneva, Lucerne, Lausanne and Basle. The principal characters with whom we are concerned were Rado (code name "Dora"), Alexander Foote ("Jim"), Edmond Hamel ("Edward") and his wife, Olga ("Maude"), Schnieper ("Taylor"), Rachel Dubendorfer ("Sissy"), Otto Punter ("Pakbo") and of course Roessler ("Lucy").

Rado was a Hungarian by birth and a cartographer by training. He ran a press agency called Geopress which specialized in international affairs. He spoke six languages and was not without talent but he was not one of the Centre's best choices (his wife was made of sterner stuff) and in the end he lost his nerve, having by that time broken a number of well established rules and also defrauded the Centre of a large sum of money. He did not take to Foote and recommended Moscow to get rid of him; this, however, was refused.

The man who had most to do with the transmitting was Foote, an Englishman who had developed left-wing leanings and during two years of the Spanish Civil War served with the International Brigade. His first signal to Moscow was sent on 20th March 1941, and the most active period was between June 1941 and October 1943 during which a total of more than 6,000 signals was passed to and from the Centre.[3]

Hamel had a wireless shop in Geneva and undertook the construction of a suitable short-wave transmitter of which eventually three were made. The Hamel couple were based on Geneva, along with Rado and a girl called Margarete Bolli ("Rose") who became Rado's mistress. Foote was based on Lausanne and Roessler on Lucerne. According to Foote, one Anna, a cut-out (go-between or middle-man), was based on Basle, but she did not play a major part in events.

Punter was a noteworthy character. He was not a full-blooded Communist but might be described as something close to a fellow traveller. He was a skilful cryptographer and he had a useful contact named Salter whose identity was not known to Foote who thought he might be a Yugoslav. In fact he was John Salter, the British agent who provided a link with Allen Dulles, then head of American Intelligence in Switzerland.[4]

These various members did not all know one another, this being in accordance with normal security procedure. Thus Foote never met Roessler until it was all over and the network practically finished.

Foote must have been a man of extraordinary stamina, for on occasion he would be content to snatch a few hours' sleep in his clothes. Transmission began at midnight and lasted till dawn, sometimes as late as nine a.m. During much of the day he was doing other work, collecting information and enciphering it, and he undertook the organization of arrangements for the transfer of funds from the Centre via America, the Centre being unable to manage this themselves. The amount of work he put in was prodigious and he certainly earned the four decorations which he was to be awarded by Moscow. When he had an hour or two to him-self, he usually rested but sometimes he would spend it with acquaintances who had nothing to do with the network and was inevitably mistaken for a war-shirker. On occasion, however, he was asked if he was a spy and would answer with a smile that he was and that his job was to look after the invisible ink.[5] When later he was arrested, those who had met him were surprised to learn that this good natured Englishman had really been an agent.

Sometimes the wave-length was changed, but such regular transmissions were, as we know, contrary to accepted security procedure, although they did not run the risk that they did in enemy-occupied territory. He was given a code group to use, meaning: "Urgent. Decipher immediately".

At first Foote could not believe that he was really working with the Russians, his doubts arising from the inefficiency of the operator at the Centre.[6] The bungling of the adminis-tration remained a source of amazement to him and to others in the network, and he later formed the opinion that success was attributable, not to the Centre, but to the agents themselves.[7]

One of the earlier signals conveyed the warnings of the attack to be launched on Russia. It was transmitted by Rado who at first was doubtful about doing so but was urged by Foote to advise the Centre. It read as follows:

Dora to Director via Taylor. Hitler definitely fixed D Day for attack on the Soviet Union on June 22. Hitler reached decision two days ago. Report received here via diplomatic courier of Swiss General Staff today. Will continue. 0130. Dora.

This was not, as we know, a unique warning. Stalin received the same warning from Sorge in Japan, from Trepper in Brussels, from Harnack in Berlin, from Sir Stafford Cripps, the British Ambassador in Moscow and, we are told, from Cordell Hull in Washington. He ignored it, probably suspecting that it had been planted by the British.

The Centre naturally wanted to know who "Lucy" was and where he got his information from, but Rado did not know the answer. Lucy merely referred to his source by the fictitious name of "Werther".

Though at first there were doubts about whether Lucy could be a genuine and trustworthy source, Stalin soon learnt to appreciate the value of the intelligence he received from the Swiss network, for Lucy's material which comprised most of it was given top priority and was sent to Lieutenant-General Golikov who passed it to Stalin personally. Lucy was awarded the handsome monthly salary of 1,700 US dollars. (It was customary for payments to Russian agents to be calculated and made in US dollars.[8])

The information obtained by Lucy and passed on to the Centre, sometimes hour by hour,[9] covered virtually everything that Moscow could have wanted to know: the strength and composition of the German Armies and Air Force, numbers of men, tanks, guns, aircraft, deployment and movements of formations and, most valuable of all, detailed plans and orders of battle. The extraordinary speed and punctuality of this intelligence naturally made Moscow wonder if it could really be genuine or if it was a plant. It seemed too good, too comprehensive and too up-to-date to be true. Rado was instructed to find out Lucy's source of information. But Lucy declined to reveal it: it was his source and he was telling nobody. Take it or leave it.

The coverage of Lucy's information was extraordinary. Though mostly concerned with military matters, it also included information about naval affairs and even about flying bombs (V1s, nicknamed "doodlebugs") and rockets (V2s).[10] So far as Stalin was concerned, he was kept supplied with information which might have come from invisible men at the headquarters of the German High Command, Air Force and Navy. On most occasions, we learn, the information was received at the Centre within twenty-four hours of it being known in Berlin.[11] Nor was that all, for sometimes Lucy was asked to obtain information: where had such-and-such a unit gone and what was its strength? In due course the answer would be forthcoming. As Foote remarked, in the end the Russian High Command very largely fought their war with Germany on the strength of Lucy's intelligence.

During this time Lucy was also keeping Swiss Intelligence posted with what concerned them, so that in effect he was operating for the Kremlin with the tacit consent of the Swiss General Staff.[12]

All went well apart from two occasions. The first occurred when the Centre suddenly went off the air without warning in the middle of a message. Foote could not understand why he could get no response. He consulted Rado. Night after night they kept trying but had no success in re-establishing contact. Rado contemplated switching to Britain. Then suddenly, after a break of nearly six weeks, the Centre resumed transmission, completing the broken message as though nothing had happened.[13] During that period the Centre had been moved from Moscow to Kuibyshev; they had not troubled to keep their Swiss network posted. Thereafter, however, normal service was resumed and information about the enemy, his strength, movements and plans, continued to be posted.

The other occasion occurred in May 1942 when Timoshenko unsuccessfully attempted to recapture Kharkov. On this isolated occasion the information provided by Lucy proved to be wrong and after the war, when Foote was in Moscow, he was told that it had cost the Russians 100,000 men. This defeat shook the Russian High Command. Maisky, the Russian Ambassador, left no doubt when he saw Eden two months later, that the position on the Eastern Front was grave.[14] For a time Russian faith in Lucy sagged. It even suggested that he might be a double agent, working for the Germans but, as is now known, it was the only occasion when Lucy's information was false, so that that suspicion does not hold water.

Foote, meantime, had been approached by a couple, George and Joanna Wilmer ("Lorenz" and "Laura") who affected to be working for the Russians but in fact had gone over to the Germans.[15] A shrewd judge of character, Foote was not taken in; they got nothing out of him.

While the Lucy network was proceeding with its task, feeding information to the Russians, Margarete Bolli, Rado's mistress, met an attractive young man calling himself Hans Peters, a hair-dresser in Geneva. In fact he was a German espionage agent and she, unlike Lucy, could not keep a secret. She mentioned to him that a German novel by Grete von Urbanitzsky was being used to provide the key for signals and named it, demonstrating that those who cannot keep things to themselves have no business to be in the service. It was fortunate that, even with this information the enemy's cryptanalysts apparently made no headway.

The extent to which the Russians depended on the intelligence provided by Lucy is evident from the demands they made. The following is a selection of signals sent from the Centre:[16]

9th November 1942:

Where are the rearward defensive positions of the Germans on the line South West of Stalingrad and along the Don?

and later the same day:

Where are now the 11th and 18th Panzer Divisions and 25th Motorized Division which were formerly employed on Bryansk sector?

2nd December 1942:

Top priority task in the near future is the most accurate determination of all German reserves in the rear of the Eastern Front.

16th January 1943:

Lucy's and Werther's information about Caucasian front and all top priority information about Eastern front, as well as despatch of new divisions to Eastern front, to be sent to us without delay with precedence over all other information. Last information from Werther most valuable.

16th February 1943:

Find out at once from Werther through Lucy whether Vyazma and Rzhev are being evacuated.

22nd February 1943:

Immediately get Werther OKW plans about objectives of Kluge's Army Group.

Lucy's answers were forthcoming; they were never more valuable than prior to the Battle of Kursk, known as "Operation Citadel". It had of course been anticipated that in the spring or early summer the enemy, who were comparatively immobile in the winter,* would launch an offensive. It was on 15th April 1943 that Hitler signed his order for Operation Citadel. In the days following, the Centre received advice:

20th April 1943:

Date for offensive against Kursk, originally visualized for the first week of May, has been postponed.

29th April 1943:

New D-Day for German offensive is 12th June.

Hitler several times postponed this offensive against the advice of his generals. It was to be the turning point in the war, a crushing defeat of the Russians which, in Hitler's words, was to "shine like a beacon to the world".[18]

In addition to providing on 9th May a full briefing of the plans for "Operation Citadel", Lucy also submitted a long and detailed inventory of the mobilization strength of the Germans, with numbers of men fit to serve, numbers called up, transfers, volunteer recruits and even juvenile volunteers, local defence battalions, men fit for garrison duty only, labour duties and serving with the Todt Organization. That information was sent on 17th April.

On 11th May Hitler again postponed "Operation Citadel", this time to 5th July, and the Russians were so advised by Lucy. On 30th May the Centre sent the following signal to Rado:

Give urgent order to Lucy to find out (1) at what point on the South sector of the Eastern front the German offensive will actually begin, (2) with what forces and in what direction will the advance be led, and (3) besides the Southern sector where and when a German offensive is planned on the Eastern front.

Fully briefed and with sufficient time provided by Hitler's postponements, the Russians seized the opportunity to

---

* The Germans wore leather boots which are said to have been a death-trap in the extreme cold; they must have noticed that the Siberian troops whom they met in their first winter wore felt ones.[17] They also found that often they could not use their wireless because the batteries had frozen.

prepare for what was to be the biggest battle on the Eastern front. It was not unexpected that the enemy would attack on the area of Kursk, about 100 miles North of Kharkov, because the Russians had recovered ground there, occupying a salient, to which the classic reaction was to attack the two flanks simultaneously. Von Kluge was to attack from the North and von Manstein from the South. Forewarned, as they were, the Russians assembled massive concentrations of troops, in particular developing fortified strongholds at Oboyan, about twenty-four miles South of Kursk, and at Malarchangelsk, a smaller town about twenty-eight miles North of Kursk. In three months of intensive preparations numerous bridges were built, nearly 1,900 miles of road and railway repaired and made usable and trenches, bunkers and mine-fields laid, and a colossal assembly of tanks, guns and flame-throwers.[19] In fact the Russians moved to this area approximately 40 per cent of their field armies, including almost all their motorized forces.[20]

These operations may have taken the enemy by surprise but it is evident that they were aware of some of them, for on 13th May Dora sent the following advice to the Centre:

German reconnaissance has identified Soviet concentrations near Kursk, Vyazma and Velikiye Luki.

On 10th June Dora sent another signal about von Manstein's order of 28th May to the motorized formations of the Fourth Panzer Army. The most remarkable of the signals, however, was one from the Centre to Dora, sent on 12th June. It read as follows:

Instruct Lucy and collaborators to establish all data about heavy tank named Panther. Important points: construction of this tank and technical characteristics, strength of armour. Is it equipped for flame-throwers and for smoke-screen laying? Location of factories manufacturing this tank. Monthly output figures.

The remarkable thing about this request was that Moscow knew at that date of the existence of this tank which was highly secret and had not been seen by any German soldiers.[21] It was as well that the Russians did have warning about this heavily armoured tank which threw flames seventy yards at a temperature of 1,000° centigrade.

The scale of operations was prodigious. Thus von Manstein's aircraft required no fewer than sixteen airfields to accommodate them.[22] Just how many tanks were involved in the biggest clash of heavy armour known is a question. Estimates have put the total as high as 15,000, which seems unlikely. The Russians suffered heavy casualties; on von Manstein's sector of the front alone these are said to have numbered 85,000 men with a further 34,000 prisoners.[23] But the German Panzer divisions were bled white. What was intended to be a great victory for them became a decisive defeat, and for once Hitler gave the order to retreat. It came at a time when for the Axis powers the tide was turning, for simultaneously the Allies took Sicily and later in the same month Mussolini was dismissed and arrested and Italy surrendered.*

If we take into account all the other battles on the Eastern front, the intelligence service maintained by Lucy was certainly prodigious.

Meantime German suspicions that Moscow was being briefed from Switzerland resulted in direction-finders being brought into action. Owing to the mountainous nature of the country, they had difficulty pin-pointing transmitting centres, but indications were that there were three, one in Geneva itself, one probably on the French side of Geneva and a third at Lausanne.[25] The Germans called the network Rote Drei (Red Three). Suspicions were strengthened when it was noticed that the Swiss Consul in Cologne made frequent and often sudden journeys to Switzerland, travelling in a courier's department of the train and carrying a black briefcase. An attempt to get the briefcase from him was unsuccessful, as it was chained to his wrist.[26]

---

* On 11th January 1944 Ciano was ignominiously tied to a chair and shot in the back; according to Hitler's interpreter, this was done on the orders of his father-in-law.[24] King Victor Emmanuel fled on 9th September 1944. Mussolini who had been rescued by the Germans on 12th September 1943 fell into the hands of partisans on 28th April 1945 and was shot on the shore of Lake Como along with his faithful mistress, Claretta Petacci, who had insisted on being with him to the last. Hitler committed suicide in his bunker on 30th April 1945.

The possibility loomed of Germany attacking Switzerland. The Swiss General Staff kept their army on the alert; the troops were well trained and well armed but, if the Germans had struck, the result could hardly have been in doubt. The Swiss authorities no doubt thought it as well to make at least a show of neutrality, and at 1.30 a.m. on 20th November 1943 Foote was arrested in his flat. Lucy was arrested on 19th May 1944. Neither Punter nor Rado were arrested. In fact no proceedings were instituted. As a demonstration of Switzerland's neutrality it sufficed. On 6th September of that year Lucy was released and Foote two days later.

For practical purposes this was the end of the network in Switzerland; though Punter made an attempt to carry on, the problem of providing funds was still outside the competence of the Centre.

Both Foote and Rado were called to Moscow and on 6th January 1945 they left in a Dakota; though Foote did not know it (for in his book he mentions the other passengers) this seems to have been the same flight which carried Trepper. The aircraft stopped at Cairo for a few days and Rado who was nervous and expected to be called to account, decided to go no further, leaving Foote to go on alone. Rado had broken practically every standard precaution; he had deposited with Hamel his secret papers and even his cipher book which fell into the hands of the Swiss Police, he had been in touch with a British agent – by itself enough to condemn him – he had taken Margarete Bolli to be his mistress, thus mixing pleasure with business, and he had embezzled perhaps as much as 50,000 dollars. The Russians applied to the British in Cairo to arrest him and hand him over which they did. He was sentenced to twenty-five years in prison; he was, however, released after Stalin's death and, when last heard of, held a post on the staff of Budapest University, his home ground.[27] Foote cleared himself in Moscow, but it was two years before he succeeded in secretly leaving the country. He returned to England and, not being in any way prevented from so doing by the Official Secrets Act, wrote a book called *Handbook for Spies* in which he told his story. It was not received with the credit it deserved. Three years after the war Punter appeared at a meeting of

Swiss Socialist editors and gave them a talk about his experience with the Lucy network; at the time he was not believed either.[28] Since then it has been acknowledged that their stories were not fictitious, and Foote's book has been translated into every major European language with, of course, the exception of Russian.

The Russian régime has not been noted for its appreciation of services rendered during the lifetime of agents. Foote himself says that it was "entirely ruthless, with no sense of honour, obligation or decency towards its servants".[29] Loathsome as the Nazi régime was, Foote thought the Russian one no better; he was thoroughly disillusioned.

It is, therefore, all the more remarkable that Lucy was one agent who received such thanks and appreciation from Moscow. Professor Dallin quotes a number of signals sent by them, bearing this out.[30] The following is a selection:

16th January 1943:

> Transmit without delay, ahead of any other messages, Lucy's and Werther's information on Caucasus front and on the important events on the Eastern front. Werther's last information very important.

22nd February 1943:

> Convey to Lucy our appreciation for good work. Last information of her group was important and valuable.

4th June 1943:

> Convey to Lucy and Long* our thanks for their work.

24th November 1943:

> Please tell Lucy on our behalf he should not worry. The transmissions to us of his information will continue and his group will receive payment without fail. We are prepared to pay amply for his information in accordance with his request.

These signals were all sent by the Director.

*   *   *   *

* The code name of Georges Blun, a French Communist.

We cannot really compare the Swiss network with others which were operated by Russia, for circumstances were quite different. The Rote Kapelle worked in the most hazardous conditions in enemy occupied territory with the threat from direction-finders amounting virtually to a certainty. In Japan Sorge, to whom we shall be coming, operated in considerably less dangerous conditions than the Rote Kapelle but, skilful as he was, he was not able to provide the same running intelligence about all Germany's military plans. The Swiss ring operated in a traditionally neutral country in conditions which could not have been easier or more convenient. In effect it was a post office.

The only thing remarkable about it is the extraordinary intelligence service it provided. It was unique, for it was continuous, detailed, punctual and, with one exception, accurate. It told the Russians at least once every twenty-four hours, and sometimes more than once, what the enemy were going to do, how they were proposing to do it and with what forces. It could fairly be said that the Russians directed the greater part of their military planning on Lucy's information, supported over a limited period by the Rote Kapelle. It was only in the very early stages before they had satisfied themselves about his credibility, and in the later stages when Germany had already lost the war, though fighting still remained to be done, that the Russians did without Lucy's information. Considering the struggle they had, with a fatal casualty roll running into millions, we may well wonder how they would have managed without Lucy.

All the members of the Swiss ring worked hard, none harder than Foote who sometimes laboured round the clock. But it was Lucy who obtained the information and, in a sense, it was he who made the network.

The one thing that nobody can explain for certain is how Lucy got hold of his intelligence. Even where we have the advice of somebody who was a participant, interviewed after the war, we may sometimes take leave to question what we are told. Rado, who was questioned by Bruce Norman, suggested that Lucy's intelligence came from the Finnish Embassy in Berlin, or from a lawyer in Leipzig with army connections, or even that he pinched it from the Swiss intelligence service.[31] So he did not know. Janusz Piekalkiewicz interviewed Marc Payot, the Swiss criminologist and cryptanalyst, whose services were used during investigations into the network's activities. What Payot had to say is interesting but in certain respects it is unhelpful.[32]

While Lucy himself said hardly anything, he maintained that he had wireless contacts which is no more than one would expect. Piekalkievicz reports that Lucy never had a wireless operator and that seems certain. He says that Lucy himself was incapable of transmitting in morse or in cipher and he also argues that no illegal wireless communication was discovered in Germany itself after 1942, that is to say before plans for the Battle of Kursk were drawn up.

If this is correct, how was the information transmitted to Lucy and who transmitted it? Even if he had got it from John Salter, the British agent in Switzerland, there would have had to be some method of communication between them. Foote tells us that there was no question of any courier or safe hand route.[33] A second question arises: when Lucy was asked to obtain information, to whom did he apply?

There have been various ideas about Lucy's source of information, but no conclusion emerges which answers all the questions. We must assume that, irrespective of what has been said of Lucy's limitations, wireless was the means of communication. At least some of the information came from East Prussia and was received in Switzerland within a few hours. The telephone was so carefully watched, with every call heard, that we can rule that out as a method.[34]

Foote says that such information could have originated only within the German High Command. Since no other body, apart from Hitler's own entourage, possessed the information, that conclusion seems beyond dispute. Every precaution must surely have been taken. Indeed Gehlen tells us that he and Canaris "repeatedly observed, independently of one another, that the enemy was receiving rapid and detailed information on incidents and top-level decision-making on the German side".[35] Tracking parties with close-range direction-finders were constantly at work, especially round Hitler's own headquarters. Yet after 1942 they found no trace of illicit traffic. Assuming that the information was sent by the approved service, implying at least one person in the High Command involved in the conspiracy, it is still difficult to see how it was done. The operator would of course be given the enciphered signal; he would not know what it meant or to whom it was addressed. Given that the recipient in Switzerland knew the frequency, he could have read it. But transmitted signals had all to be logged, somebody had to acknowledge receipt, which in turn had to be checked by an authorized person.[36]

Foote did not meet Lucy till his release from prison, when through a cut-out Lucy expressed a wish to meet him. Foote of course agreed. He found Lucy a rather insignificant looking little man and tells us that the only clue Lucy gave him was when he said that the purge which followed the unsuccessful attempt on Hitler's life in July 1944 had considerably reduced the number of his sources. Foote adds that the almost complete elimination of any potential resistance movement had obviously merely embarrassed Lucy and temporarily inconvenienced him but had not removed his sources *in toto*.[37]

For want of some kind of identity reference during the war, the source was referred to as "Werther", the only name by which Foote knew it from earliest days. That might conceal the name of an individual. If that is so, however, it suggests somebody who had continuous access to practically every secret of the German High Command. Hitler had plenty of enemies in his own country, many of them in high places, and it is of course possible that somebody managed to evade the purge and continued to perform the task of feeding Lucy with information and also of answering his questions. If that is so, one would like to know the means he used to transmit it and to answer Lucy's questions over such a long period without being discovered.

Paul Karl Schmidt, a member of the German diplomatic corps who later, under the name of Paul Carell, wrote some excellent histories of the war on the Eastern front, considered whether the Swiss Secret Service, through their man, Major Hausamann, could have obtained the information from a source named "Teddy" but came to the conclusion that that could not be the answer. For one thing, Hausamann's information was not identical with Lucy's and, so far as the Battle of Kursk is concerned, was incorrect.[38]

Two Frenchman, Accoce and Quet, put forward the idea that the service was provided by a group of Bavarian officers, apparently numbering ten in all.[39] One of them was said to be General Thiele who was in charge of the High Command's signal service. It need hardly be said that no other service was more closely watched by the secret police. If ten men really succeeded in this task over a period of four years, not one of them putting a foot wrong, it was certainly a remarkable feat and, human nature being what it is, we would have expected at least one of them afterwards proudly to proclaim the achievement and remove doubts about how it was done.

A quite different answer to the question was later suggested by Malcolm Muggeridge.[40] This was that the information was provided by our own SIS. At the time it naturally posed the question: how did SIS themselves get hold of all this intelligence with every detail of the enemy's plans for the Eastern front, with a daily service of everything the Russian High Command could want? In the last week of October 1974, however, publication of the book *The Ultra Secret* by F. W. Winterbotham told the world how we read Enigma signals used throughout the German High Command. That made Muggeridge's idea more feasible, given that there were no periods when we were unable to read the relevant signals. Certainly it would have been a good way of feeding to Stalin information which, if it had come direct from us, might have been regarded as suspect. Though we regarded the Russians as our Allies and there were meetings of heads of governments, Russian prejudice was so strong that any question of having truck with SIS was apparently ruled out, so far as Moscow was concerned.

We would not have passed to the Russians the most precious of our secrets, the key to Enigma which would have meant presenting them with the bronze goddess; and on the assumption that we could have read all the relevant signals, the possibility arises that we fed the information.

Calvocoressi who himself worked at Bletchley tells us that

we gave the Russians Ultra information direct but without revealing its source, in particular before the battles in the summer of 1942, but that the advice was not heeded. We were aware of the quite inadequate standard of security in the Russian signals service (which we have noted in the story of the Rote Kapelle) and could not afford to reveal the source of our intelligence lest the Russians in turn unwittingly give it away. For our reading of Enigma signals left us in no doubt that the Germans were reading Russian signals.

It has been said by others that the Russians had broken Enigma by 1942, but that is difficult to reconcile with their scepticism about our Ultra information. Moreover, if the Russians were really reading Enigma except during the early months of the war on the Eastern front, why should they waste their time and money depending on Lucy – if he in turn was dependent on Ultra – when they could get it all direct for themselves? Moreover, if this were the answer, Lucy's source (he used the word "sources") would not have been affected by the purge which followed the unsuccessful attempt on Hitler's life in July 1944. The theory that we fed the information *via* Lucy – who would thus have been no more than a cut-out – does not wash. What we fed to the Russians was fed direct. Apart from that, it leaves unanswered the question: when requests were received from Moscow by Lucy to ascertain the whereabouts of a particular unit of the German army and its strength, or detailed figures of the enemy's man-power, call-up of reserves and so on, to whom were they referred? There must have been a voice, and it is the identity of that voice that we do not know. There may no longer be anybody alive who does know.

Was there really a Russian agent in the German High Command, a "Werther" or a number of them? After all, Russian agents seem to have penetrated all sorts of quarters. In our own Foreign Office there was one in the Communications Department in 1939;[42] and in Germany they seem to have penetrated every government department and even the most secret organizations, as we noted from the position occupied by Heinz Felfe (page 93). Did someone – or perhaps more than one – on the German High Command succeed in continuing to transmit intelligence and to answer inquiries despite the most thorough precautions taken by the Germans to prevent it?

Paul Schmidt, who spent some time pursuing research into the problem, confessed himself defeated by this question, and he draws attention to one instance which he found staggering. On the afternoon of 28th March 1942 there was a top secret conference at Hitler's headquarters. Three days later an abstract of the discussion was being studied by a Swiss general in Berne; and on the following day it was transmitted to the Centre with the usual opening, "Dora to Director"[43] How did they get hold of that information?

We know the identities of all those who used cover names with the solitary exception of "Werther". There must have been such a voice. Who was he? Two people once knew the answer, "Werther" himself and Lucy. The Russians did not know, for Lucy declined to reveal the identity of his source. If anyone who once knew is still alive, he would surely have told us by now, if he had been going to talk. It is tempting to pronounce an *ipse dixit,* but it cannot carry conviction unless we know how it was done, for there are questions to which at present there are no answers. There is nothing surprising in that, for in highly secret work it is inevitably common enough; and when we do not know, it is surely sensible and right to acknowledge it.

Wherever Lucy got his information from, and to whom he directed his inquiries, he told nobody. He kept his secret and, as Punter said with approval, took it with him to the grave. R.I.P.

SIX

HERO OF THE SOVIET UNION
Richard Sorge in Japan

With the exception of Mata Hari, probably more romantic nonsense has been written about Richard Sorge, the Russian agent in Japan, than about any other agent in modern times.

Sorge's mother was Russian and his father a German, but much about his family background is uncertain. It is, however, known that he served in the German Army in the First World War and was wounded, and that afterwards he became a miner in the Rhineland. He became an active Communist, creating Communist cells both in the pits where he began working and in those in the Dutch province of Limburg. In 1920 he joined the Communist Party. In the following year he married Christiane Gerlach who had been married to a Professor Gerlach. There does not seem to have been any bad blood between the two men; Sorge wanted her and she wanted him, so her husband obliged both of them by obtaining a divorce. In fact her marriage to Sorge did not last and later there was a divorce, also an amicable one.

Sorge attended the Sixth Congress of the Comintern in 1923 and in the following year was recruited into the Comintern Intelligence Service. Five years later he was posted to Military Intelligence.[1] He was sent to China and he set up a spy ring in Shanghai. He returned to Moscow in 1933 and was then posted to Japan, staying *en route* in Germany for some months during which he managed to obtain a German passport. By the time he arrived in Yokohama, he was the accredited special correspondent of the *Frankfurter Zeitung*.

In Tokyo Sorge quickly made his number with the German Embassy where he met Colonel Ott, the Military Attaché, and they soon got onto friendly terms. Sorge knew that he was likely to be watched by the police and he took his time setting up his spy ring. In December 1933 Dr Hubert von Dircksen took up his post as Ambassador and he too found Sorge an interesting character. Sorge showed himself to be a mixture. He was a heavy drinker and could be coarse and offensive, particularly when in his cups, but he could also be charming when he chose. It was accepted that, as a journalist, he should be interested in news of all kinds. He soon took his place in the German colony; nobody thought he was other than what he professed to be, an intelligent gatherer of news, vulgar or pleasant as the mood took him, given to raising the elbow rather too often perhaps, but a direct character who knew his job and got on with it.

Sorge made contact with a young Communist from Croatia, Branko Vukelic.[2] The latter was hard up and Sorge gave him some money. A photo technician by training, Vukelic was quickly earmarked for the network, to be followed in 1934 by Hotsumi Ozaki, another Communist whom Sorge had met in China, a close friend of Prince Konoye, the Prime Minister, an acquaintance of General Ugoye, and like Sorge a newspaper correspondent. A third recruit was known as "Bernhard" who was supposed to operate the transmitter; he did not send many signals, being nervous of being caught and Sorge asked Moscow to recall him. His successor, Max Klausen, was a more suitable character; a German Communist on the payroll of Moscow, he had met Sorge earlier and in 1935 was sent to Japan to join him. A trained wireless technician, he set himself up in a small company as a cover.

So far as is known, Sorge's communications with Moscow began in 1934 and until the middle of 1935 were sent by courier. He cultivated his friendship with Ott with whom he was soon on terms of confidence, and von Dircksen apparently found him acceptable. In fact Sorge became almost a major-domo to Ott; on one occasion Ott asked him to encode a signal for him and Sorge of course made a photo-copy of the code which he sent to Moscow by courier. All went well during this period and when in 1938 von Dircksen's term of office ended, Ott, then a Major-

General, succeeded him. By this time Sorge had added to his spy-ring twelve sub-agents or informants.[3]

Before this time Sorge had met a young waitress named Miyake Hanako who became devoted to him.[4] At no time did she suspect his secret activities. Indeed she brought out the best in Sorge. In so far as he was capable, he seems to have returned her love, for he was kind and gentle to her. This was Sorge at his best and most human.

In his communications with the Centre Sorge followed the usual practice of using a cipher with a constantly changing key, with groups of numerals to which others of a random nature were added. The source from which the random figures were obtained was the *German Statistical Year Book*; as this was commonly to be found in households of the German colony, its presence would arouse no surprise or suspicion in the unlikely event of the house being searched. Klausen did the transmitting for him.

By this time a further member had been recruited to the espionage network, one Yotoku Miyagi, together with a number of sub-agents. Klausen did not cultivate the German Embassy but met Sorge at the German Club in Tokyo. On occasion he would visit him at his home but these visits were not intended to be known to others and the arrangement was that, if on arrival Klausen found the gate lamp lit, he would know that Sorge already had a visitor and he himself would not then enter.

Sorge was by this time having difficulties with the Centre who directed that his total expenditure was not to exceed 1,000 dollars a month, a maximum that was later reduced to about half of what Roessler was alone paid in Lucerne. Traditionally Moscow did not pay particularly high salaries to their agents, as it was undesirable that they should attract attention to themselves by lavish expenditure. But in this case they went further and directed that Klausen was to reduce the profits which he made from his cover company. In return Klausen reduced the amount he transmitted. He carried his transmitter in a leather bag but had one or two hair-raising incidents. On one occasion he left his wallet in a taxi; it contained a report in English for transmission to Moscow. However, he heard no more about it.[5]

Sorge's superiors at the Centre did not show much understanding of the practical problems of operating a spy ring
and the need to build it up with caution. They were impa-
tient to receive more high-level intelligence. Twice in one day
they rebuked him for not being more informative. At that
stage Sorge was no hero of the Soviet Union.

With the outbreak of war Sorge, ostensibly a German
subject, became more closely associated with the Embassy.
During April and May 1941 the diplomatic couriers noticed
movements of Army units towards the Soviet frontier. In
May Sorge advised the Centre that Hitler had sent Hess to
Britain in a last effort to reach a peaceful agreement. He also
sent to Moscow a microfilm of a telegram from von Ribbentrop to Ott, giving an approximate date for the forthcoming attack on Russia; and on 15th May he followed it up
by giving the exact day. In fact Sorge's messages to Moscow
were thoroughly sound, even if they were not always
appreciated. We are told that in 1940 alone he transmitted
to the Centre 30,000 enciphered word groups.[6] By the
autumn of the following year Sorge was able to assure
Moscow that there was no danger of a Japanese attack on
Russia; this was his outstanding contribution, enabling
Stalin to transfer his troops from his Eastern front and throw
them into the fight against Germany. But Japan's intentions
regarding America and South-East Asia were another matter. These, however, had not been translated into action by
the time Sorge's career as an espionage agent came to a
sudden and unexpected end.

In November 1939 the Japanese Police began a drive
aimed at breaking up the construction of a Communist
party. In the course of subsequent developments they
arrested one Ito Ritsu, with whom Ozaki had links. They
also sought Yotoku Miyagi who lodged with a Mrs. Tomo
Kitabayashi, an obscure dress-maker who was never more
than a minor informant. They took her away for questioning
and she, in her innocent way, apparently assumed that her
lodger, Miyagi, was also under arrest and talked freely in so
far as she had anything material to contribute. Miyagi's
arrest followed on 11th October 1941. He admitted being a
member of the espionage network consisting principally of

Sorge, Vukelic, Klausen and Ozaki. In operating the ring Sorge had evidently allowed too many members to know the identity of others. Thus the whole network was undermined, and even the position of the Prime Minister, Prince Konoye, was called in question.

At first the procurator was doubtful about the case against Sorge who meantime was awaiting Ozaki at a pre-arranged meeting. Klausen was then present with Sorge. When Ozaki did not appear, Klausen became nervous. When he left Sorge's house, he realized that he was being shadowed and the next day he was arrested. On the same day, 23rd October 1941, Sorge was also detained. His house was searched. Though the procurator had had considerable doubts about whether Sorge could be guilty, they were removed when the police reported having found three cameras, a copying camera with accessories, three photo lenses, one of them telescopic, a number of notebooks containing identities of contacts and of expenditure, a list of Communist Party members in Japan, several pages of reports and other material in English, and two pages of a typed draft in English of a message to be sent to Moscow.[7] If anyone had been intent on framing Sorge, he could not have astonished the police with a more damning display of evidence.

Both Klausen and Vukelic had by this time turned against Communism, the former perhaps influenced by his wife who had always disliked it. Their awakening, however, came too late to save either of them. Klausen under arrest did not make much of a fight of it and soon confessed. Sorge's confession followed.

Japanese legal procedure is a long drawn out process. First there is questioning at a police station, followed by an investigation at a detention centre. Both these two processes can be prolonged. The final stage, the trial, is little more than a formality and bears no resemblance to a British court of justice, because the relevant evidence has already been ascertained.

Both Klausen and Vukelic were sentenced to life imprisonment. Klausen was nearly burnt to death in his cell during an air attack by American bombers. During his time in gaol his weight fell by five and a half stone.[8] He survived and was later released. Vukelic died in prison in the frozen wastes at Abashiri in January 1945.

Both Sorge and Ozaki were sentenced to death on 29th September 1943. The sentence came as a shock to Sorge, who had expressed himself as willing to spy for the Japanese.[9] His appeal on 20th January 1944 failed. The execution was, however, delayed till the following November, being timed to take place on the twenty-seventh anniversary of the Russian Revolution.

In the years since then the legend has been fostered that Sorge somehow managed to escape and that somebody else obligingly took his place. The story is, however, without foundation. The executioner later stated that he had seen Sorge exercising in the prison yard and had no doubt at all that the man he had hanged was Sorge. Miyake Hanako later examined his remains, recognized the gold fillings in certain of his teeth and had them removed to be made into a ring for her; she also noted the fracture in the bones of one leg, as a result of a wound sustained in the First World War. She too was in no doubt about the identity of the man who had been hanged.

The possibility has also been raised that Sorge was a double agent, spying for both Germany and Russia. That makes more sense in that as a special correspondent of a German newspaper he was sending information to Germany, but it is doubtful if there was any more to it than that.

That Sorge was a valuable agent is not in question. But he became careless as well as cocky in his cups, as was demonstrated by the abundant proof of his guilt which he left for the police to find in his house; and too many in the network knew who the others were.

In September 1965, almost twenty-one years after his death and nearly twenty-four years after his arrest, Sorge was posthumously made a "Hero of the Soviet Union"; a street in Moscow was named after him and later a tanker. In addition a four kopek stamp was issued bearing his head, and later still a play was written about him. It is not explained why the Russian authorities took so long to discover that he was a hero.

As a footnote to this story, it may be added that Miyake

Hanako, his faithful girl-friend, had his body removed and buried in a cemetery with a tombstone bearing his name, and there she was often to be seen in prayer, her gold ring on her finger.

SEVEN

AMERICAN MAGIC
How Japan was Outwitted

Of the major powers that participated in the Second World War the one that was least equipped by experience to compete in the hidden war of ciphers and codes was Japan. It is not clear why she was late coming into the field; by contrast the origin of Chinese codes goes back to the eleventh century.[1] Not only were Japan's rivals long in the tooth where ciphers were concerned, with centuries of experience behind them, but though we tend to think of cipher machines as modern, the first patents taken out in most of the leading countries date back to the nineteenth century.[2] Japan, however, lagged behind.

After the end of the First World War the Japanese engaged the services of a Polish expert, Captain (later Colonel) Jan Kowalewsky, to improve their standard of cipher work, lecturing to their cadets on the construction of ciphers and their unravelment. From him they learnt what makes ciphers vulnerable. But it was from America that they probably obtained even greater help.

During the Twenties, when among the Western democracies disarmament was much in vogue, the American Black Chamber* which Herbert O. Yardley had operated so successfully in the First World War was closed by Henry L. Stimson, the Secretary of State, by the simple expedient of cutting off funds. He did not approve of "reading other people's mail".

Subsequently Yardley wrote a book about his experience

* The origin of this term dates back to the reign of Louis XV, whose mistress, Madame de Pompadour, set aside a room for cipher work and called it her *Chambre Noire*.

and achievements; it proved a best seller. With the help of one of his staff who spoke Japanese he had unravelled Japanese signals; and on the closure of his organization he approached the Japanese Embassy and offered his services. It is not unique for experts in cryptography who have been retired from regular employment to make themselves available as consultants and offer their services to other nations. Kowalewsky was not the first to do so after the First World War. When the French cipher chief, Brigadier-General Henri Cartier, retired in 1919, his services became available to other nations. There is no suggestion that either of these sold any of their own countries' secrets, but clearly the practice is watched with certain misgivings, for such a consultant will very probably give away something of the ways and means of his own country, if only by inference. Yardley, however, is believed to have gone further and to have sold America's secrets to the Japanese, including among others the solutions of British diplomatic ciphers known to him.[3]

With the advice of Kowalewsky and Yardley, the Japanese set about devising a system which would enable them to compete with other powers by using ciphers of an exceptionally high standard of security. This did not, of course, enable them to become skilled at unravelling others' ciphers, a field in which, as events proved, they were unable to compete; but at least it promised to provide them with a system likely to defeat attempts of others to break it. In the early Thirties they purchased the original model of the Enigma which could then be bought on the open market. It was from this that the Germans later developed the highly sophisticated machine used by their High Command.

The traditional type of cipher machine was based on the rotor system and resembled a portable electric typewriter with a drum at the back and beneath it the mechanism to do the enciphering, methodically producing a substitution series of many thousands of letters long, so varying their use that a single word would reappear in its initially enciphered form only at long intervals.

One of the elementary lessons which the Japanese had no doubt learnt was that the more a cipher is used, the weaker its security, and they therefore equipped themselves with a number of systems, switching from one to another and also introducing variants into each system. The one that became known to the Americans as Purple consisted in effect of two typewriter machines of the kind described, separated by a plugboard and a box of cipher wheels. The plugboard had a plug for each letter of the Roman alphabet (which the Japanese used for enciphering). The effect of using the double machine was an ingenious form of super-encipherment with a multitude of manipulated variations. The result was that, to break the cipher, a cryptanalyst would need to construct a machine with an identical mechanism and experiment with it.

The number of cipher alphabets of twenty-six letters available for monoalphabetic substitution ciphers is almost unbelievably huge, running into many millions.[5] The effect of multiplicity of proliferation can be better appreciated, when we remember that even words in common use occur in plain text at fairly long intervals: for example "is" occurs on an average seventy-two times in 1,000 words, "are" forty times, "on" thirty times and "we" twelve times. It follows that the Purple cipher was so able to jumble the use of letters that the recurrence of a word in the original enciphered form required perhaps hundreds of signals. It was this characteristic that made the Japanese so sure that that cipher could not be broken.

To unravel complex ciphers produced by machines, the cryptanalyst can make use of electronic devices. There are computers that perform additions of letters at an extraordinary speed;[6] and they can also be used to test for groups of letters. But in such circumstances what the cryptanalyst most needs is to examine a model of the machine.

Guarding their precious cipher carefully, the Japanese did not equip all their diplomatic offices with it; only about a dozen of their embassies were provided with them. This, however, provided America's Signals Intelligence Service, led by William F. Friedman, with a certain amount of assistance, for sometimes the same signal would be sent to all their embassies, a number of which were using systems which the Americans were already reading. Thus Friedman and his team were provided with the plain text of the signal in Purple. The most useful aid, however, may have come from a ruse whereby, ostensibly investigating a contrived failure in the electricity supply at the Japanese Embassy in Washington, two of their agents were able to take a quick look at an enciphering machine. It is believed also that a document later found in a brief case provided additional help.[7]

The task of Friedman and his staff involved experimenting with the wiring and switches of the wheels of a "shadow" machine: this in itself was complicated by the daily changes in the plugboard connections. Then the starting point for each day's signals fell to be determined. What was discovered was that the daily keys within each of a ten-day period appeared to be related; that is to say, the operators changed the keys to form those for the following nine days.[8] Eventually experimental work on the "shadow" machine produced the answer.

All this work occupied the best part of twenty months with a legacy of immense nervous strain and exhaustion. Though the breakthrough occurred a month earlier, the first fully intelligible and ungarbled text was recovered on 25th September 1940.[9] So skilful had been the construction of the "shadow" machine that signals which the Japanese were sending became available to the Americans before they were read at the Japanese Embassy. It was noted that Japanese cipher clerks often had to call upon headquarters for verification,[10] reflecting the marked difference in standards of efficiency.

We may pause to note one interesting distinction between the security of Japanese military ciphers, used immediately before Pearl Harbour, and Purple. The Americans were then unable to break the military cipher system, not because of any superiority to Purple, but because the amount of material available to them was small.[11]

Instructions were given by Roosevelt that the solutions of Purple and of other systems unravelled by the Americans were to be given to the British in exchange for British successes in reading German and Italian systems.[12] Churchill records that it was these American successes in reading Japanese signals which were referred to as "Magics", that enabled the British team to read Purple signals.[13] In January 1941 a machine for reading Purple was brought to this country.

Even with the Americans' own Signals Intelligence Service knowledge of this success in breaking Purple was confined to a limited number. Sometimes there were delays, perhaps because of changes in wave-length, sometimes garbled texts, and sometimes the sheer volume of material received.[14]

Arising from their feat in breaking Purple, the Americans were faced with the same problem that had presented itself to their Allies when they had mastered Enigma. Who was to know about it and hae copies of the deciphered text of Japanese signals? In the event regular distribution was confined to thirteen people, principally President Roosevelt, the Secretary of State, War and Navy, the Chiefs of Staff of the Army and Navy and the Intelligence and War Plans Chiefs of the Army and Navy.[15] One absentee from the regular list was Admiral Kimmel, then Commander in Chief of the Pacific Fleet at Pearl Harbour, Isle of Oahu, Hawaii.

In the first few days of December Tokyo sent out instructions to diplomatic and consular offices in various centres, including both Washington and London, that codes and cipher machines were to be destroyed[16] and that certain staff in Washington were to return home at once. These signals were ominous signs, alerting the informed that Japan was on the brink of war. Roosevelt was the head of a country that was traditionally peace-loving and accordingly decided to leave it to the Japanese to make the dclaration of war. In the event such declaration as was made was sent so late that, in effect, it was not an advance warning at all; as Japan was to show, particularly in her fiendish treatment of prisoners, she was no respecter of what are known as the rules of war. She never had been.*

Shortly before eight o'clock on the morning of 7th

---

* It is generally accepted that in 1904 it was Japan that went to war with Russia and not the other way about and did so without any declaration of war, though there had been an incident earlier that day when the Russians opened fire at Chemulpo. That night, while the Russian officers were ashore attending a ball, the Japanese torpedoed the Russian fleet which lay in a harbour at Port Arthur.

December 1941 the attack began, launched principally from Japanese aircraft carriers. In a little under two hours the battleship *Arizona* was blown up, the *Utah* and the *Oklahoma* capsized, the *West Virginia* and the *California* were sunk at their moorings, and every other naval vessel was heavily damaged, while in addition 188 American aircraft were destroyed and 128 others damaged; 2,400 Americans lost their lives.

Dusko Popov, a Yugoslav who was one of MI5's wartime agents and a fearless and adventurous character, has some direct comments to make about a warning of the attack on Pearl Harbour given to J. Edgar Hoover, head of the FBI, four months before the event.[17] Masterman's attitude, however, suggests that the full degree of trust between the British and American secret services had not then been established and amounted to a *mea culpa*. Nothing, in any case, can excuse the action of the Japanese in planning and carrying out an entirely unprovoked attack without a timely declaration of war.

It was not only in unravelling Purple that the Americans showed remarkable skill, for we learn that Commander Dyer, one of their cryptanalysts, estimated that during the war with Japan the Americans read no fewer than seventy-five Japanese cryptosystems,[18] some of them perhaps variants. The Japanese could not compete; by contrast, they could read none of the American systems.[19]

Winterbotham states that the Japanese Army, Navy and Air Force began using the sophisticated Enigma, as developed by the Germans, but does not know just when they did so. (His book was written from memory.) The reader may wonder how the Japanese came to acquire it, for it is certain that the Germans would never have handed it to an ally who was so casual about security that, when advised that Purple was being read, they did not immediately bring another system into use. They would have been unlikely to do so, even without that discouragement. Until there is an official story of the Ultra secret and more is revealed, the uninformed can do no more than speculate on the evidence already available. It will be remembered that both Germany and Japan bought the original Enigma machine when it was

on the commercial market in the early Thirties. Both
developed it into more sophisticated forms. As we have seen,
the bronze goddess (by this time Mark II) was able, with
the skill of its handlers, to keep pace with the numerous
variations made by the Germans, small ones daily and
major changes at longer intervals. Indeed the adaptability
of this electronic construction was essential to its successful
operation. It is not, therefore, so surprising that this same
device could be used to disentangle the cipher used by the
Japanese.

At all events, arrangements were put in hand for the Ultra
security system of advising those who needed to be kept
posted, both on land and at sea.[20] General Slim and the two
American military commanders, Stillwell and Chennault,
were kept posted for their purposes, as were Mountbatten
and Nimitz for naval operations. The signals provided the
same comprehensive service of essentials as they did about
the Germans.

The American Naval Commander in Chief, Admiral
Chester W. Nimitz, was soon in action after his appointment.
With the advantage of knowing in advance the intentions of
the enemy, he was able at the Battle of the Coral Sea to
defeat the threat to Port Moresby.[21] History will no doubt
record that one of the decisive engagements of the war was
the victory of the American Pacific Fleet at the Battle of
Midway. Nimitz had known the intentions of the Japanese
three weeks before the engagement in June 1942, when his
dive-bombers destroyed the entire carrier force of Admiral
Nagumo and virtually finished Japan's offensive power at
sea.[22] It is an interesting reflection on the changed form of
naval warfare that this engagement took place while the
American warships were not themselves within sight of those
of the Japanese.

The same ability to keep abreast of Japanese intentions by
reading their signals was used to bring about the death of
Admiral Yamamoto nearly a year after the Battle of Midway. Yamamoto was Commander in Chief of the Japanese
Navy, and it became known to the Americans that he would
be visiting certain of the islands in the Solomons group. It
was known also that his aircraft would be escorted by six

fighters, and the precise details of his timetable were also learnt. The Americans decided to shoot him down.

Since the Japanese might well assume from this operation that their signals were being read, a cover story was devised to the effect that watchers on the coast of Australia had obtained the information, probably from natives on Rabaul, and had passed it on to the Americans.[23] The operation nonetheless resulted in a protest from London to Washington on the grounds that the security of the Ultra service had been put at risk.[24] Fortunately, however, the fears proved groundless.* Likewise fortunately the death of Yamamoto was a blow to Japanese pride. Just as many seamen who had never seen Nelson wept when they knew of his death, so the Japanese were shaken severely when they learnt of that of their national hero.

*   *   *   *

So far as operations on land were concerned, the Americans were of course guided by the Ultra service. Whereas our own Montgomery evidently made no acknowledgement of what he owed to Ultra, both Patton and Bradley did. Montgomery was by nature disinclined to attack until he had a preponderance of arms. Patton, perhaps the ablest commander of heavy armour the Allies had, was the opposite; completely confident in the information he received from the Ultra service, he took chances which in other circumstances might well have been asking for trouble; he must have found the results singularly rewarding.

Characteristically, the Americans do not hide the fact that, when their country was brought into the war, the standard of their Intelligence Service was not what it should have been. Those of us in our own Intelligence Services who met

---

* Shortly before the Allies landed in Sicily, an incident took place which may seem comparable. It became known, through reading an Enigma signal, that Kesselring had established his headquarters there at the San Dominco Hotel. An RAF aircraft dropped a bomb on the centre of the building, causing considerable loss of life; Kesselring himself, however, was then away, apparently in Rome. The circumstances were not quite identical with those of the attack on Yamamoto, as Kesselring was anticipating the Allied invasion which followed shortly afterwards.[25]

Americans soon after their entry into the war will not have been surprised that this view was expressed by General Marshall to the Senate Committee on Military Affairs after the war; and Dean Acheson said much the same to Congress.[26] But a Congressional Inquiry into Pearl Harbour exonerated the cryptanalytic services of blame.[27] Their skill was of the highest from pre-war years. Their feat in disentangling Purple, and the British feat in solving Enigma, stand out as the two supreme achievements of skill.

EIGHT

MEN IN THE SHADOWS
Espionage and Counter Espionage

On the evidence available it seems that at the outbreak of hostilities the Germans had penetrated our latest diplomatic ciphers only in part. It is known that they had been getting rapid and accurate information about secret exchanges between London and Moscow which suggests communications from an informed source; on occasion they received it on the same day that London did. But of some important matters of which knowledge of our ciphers would have kept them informed, they were evidently ignorant.[1]

Because diplomatic establishments house important secrets, they naturally attract agents and sometimes what we might call freelances, ready to sell their discoveries to buyers; and these people are often helped by the notorious indiscretions and lack of security that seem to afflict these establishments.

"Some diplomatic representatives", we are told, "either had no training in security (that is to say, in the ways in which information can become available to and used by an enemy) or did not understand the difference between the requirements of peace and those of war."[2] It is one thing to prattle away in a memorandum to be carried by courier but quite another thing to do so in a telephone conversation or in something that is to be enciphered; for the more enciphered material the enemy has at his disposal, the better his changes of breaking the cipher.

We read that in the small hours of 31st August 1939 our own Ambassador in Berlin was secretly visited by two people, one of them Ulrich von Hassel, former German Ambassador in Rome who was anti-Hitler and therefore a leading member of the underground movement. They warned him of the imminent attack on Poland and, immediately they had left, he telephoned his own Foreign Office as well as both the Polish and French Embassies in Berlin, even though in a police state it should have been obvious that his telephone would have been tapped. The information was passed on without a thought for the safety of his two visitors.[3] The Polish Embassy would have immediately informed their Government of the meeting; if cipher had been used, it would not have helped for, as we now know, the Germans had already broken it.[4]

The British Ambassador was far from the only one whose indiscretions were a byword, for the Italian, French, Dutch, Belgian and Balkan diplomats also had the reputation of exercising little discipline when talking on the telephone.[5] Nor was the telephone the only means of committing indiscretions, for the lifting of documents carelessly left lying about, and of waste paper was common practice. Thus in his diary Ciano refers to "the usual documents" lifted from the British Embassy.[6]

In such circumstances an agent who had secured a post on the staff, not necessarily on the switchboard, perhaps merely carrying round cups of tea or drinks or emptying waste-paper baskets, could pick up information without even trying. If they could get hold of the key to the safe, they could of course have access to ciphers and codes, and the employment of experienced safe-breakers buzzed with activity. We are told that at the outbreak of war a number of these craftsmen were released from our own prisons to work for us.[7]

Espionage agents employed by a Secret Service were of course answerable to their superiors, though that did not prevent the more enterprising and less scrupulous of them from making copies of their discoveries and selling them as unauthorized side-lines. Freelance adventurers who were answerable to nobody would peddle what they had to sell in any market conveniently accessible. Those who were up bright and early in the morning were only too ready to do business with prospective buyers. ("Pist! You want nice cipher, Mister? Turkish one. Very good. Very secret. For you only £40, for anyone else £50.")

Before the Russians moved in, Riga was swarming with

agents who sat at a café opposite the Stock Exchange and carried on a broking business of their own. There were dozens of these agents to be found there; they did not scruple to sell to the highest bidder, nor at a later date to sell the same information to the opposition at an increased price. Nicholson, Britain's SIS man there, formed the view that much of the information was unreliable and surmised that some of it had been planted by the Germans or the Russians.[8] We learn, too, that Lisbon was a bee-hive of espionage agents, and Turkey was an equally active market.[9] Nor was there any shortage of these gentry in Spain or along the North African littoral.

The value of the information on sale varied widely. It might be no more than some item of news or rumour dressed up in secret wrapping, available maybe at no more than ten pounds or so, but on occasion it could be of considerable attraction and interest, and the prospective buyer had to be remarkably perceptive and discriminating. As always, judgement was the only yardstick.

On occasion diplomatic institutions themselves made a market, if the officials concerned did not feel the burden of scruples too heavy, or if loyalties, in so far as they exercised an influence, were divided. Thus Finland, though traditionally sympathetic to the Western democracies of which of course she was one, was attacked by Russia in 1939 and to some extent therefore later looked upon Germany as in the nature of an ally.*

---

* When Finland was attacked by Russia in November 1939, British sympathies with the Finns were strong, and there was support from General Ironside for sending an expeditionary force, and doing so across others' territory even without their consent. Fortunately this hare-brained idea was not adopted and four months later the Finns surrendered. On 21st June 1941 Finland was informed of the attack to be launched on Russia on the following day when Hitler announced that Finnish and German troops stood side by side. Russia replied by bombing Helsinki and the Finnish-Russian war was reopened. On 29th November 1941 Churchill wrote to Marshal Mannerheim, the Finnish President, then in his seventies, suggesting that enough territory had been recovered and that he should pull out of the war; Mannerheim replied that he could not agree.[10] Finland later had to pay a heavy price to Russia. Mannerheim was internationally much respected, and Britain's action in depriving him of his GBE in February 1942[11] seemed small as well as undeserved. In Helsinki his is the only equestrian statue.

At the Finnish Embassy in Stockholm there was an occasional market for the genuine article, and information was sold to both Allied and Axis services. Thus, from the Finnish Military Attaché Colonel (later General) Donovan's Office of Strategic Services (OSS) which was a sort of combination of our SIS AND SOE, purchased some excellent German and Russian battle order reports. The Finnish Naval Attaché made an even more rearkable sale to OSS, a complete description of the Russian Navy. On the other hand the Finns sold to the Axis powers the key to an American diplomatic code.[12] While it is possible, as has been claimed, that the Finns had themselves broken that code, it does not seem likely, for in their war with Russia lack of wireless and consequential dependence on couriers or the telephone[13] do not suggest that the Finns were well practised in cryptography. They may have obtained help from Sweden who acted as fairy godmother to her Scandinavian neighbours. They are also believed to have had personal help from Heinz Bonatz, the head of B-Dienst.[14]

The usual practice, anyway in Britain's SIS, was for agents to communicate with other agents or contacts through a cut-out and often more than one, merely on security grounds. The sums offered for information varied but could be high. Admiral Maugeri, head of Italian Naval Intelligence, had confidence in the security of their naval code, because he knew that a British agent in Switzerland maintained an open offer of £40,000 sterling for the system.[15] Whether such an offer was genuinely made we do not know, but it could have been. This may be questioned in view of the feat of Mrs Pack in late 1940 in obtaining the key to a naval code at the Italian Embassy in Washington,* an exploit that has become well known. But the one which she obtained was probably not the one used by the Italians at Cape Matapan in March 1941. We do know that, though at one time we had a

---

* An American girl, Amy Thorpe Pack, the wife of a member of the British diplomatic corps, used her charms to secure en clair nearly all the telegrams despatched by the Vichy Embassy and also the keys to Vichy and Italian naval cryptosystems.[16] In Cadogan's diary it is recorded that we were reading Italian naval signals from 1941 and both the Spanish and Vichy diplomatic ones from 1942.[17]

reputation of being a bit mean with our bids, we could make generous offers for what we badly wanted. In Riga, we are told, offers were high enough to attract even a rich man, and the offer for a German War Office cipher was so high that "it would have made a saint's mouth water".[18]

The use of agents to obtain the keys to ciphers and codes became one of their most fruitful activities. A British agent is believed to have obtained the key to the code used in the Italian submarine service, leading to the sinking of a number of these vessels.[19]

General Cesare Amé, head of the Italian Secret Service, made good use of espionage agents to obtain the keys to ciphers and codes. We learn from him that, with the solitary exception of the Russian Embassy, he had keys to all the embassies in Rome.[20] From his own window he could watch the United States Embassy where he had two agents, employees on the American staff. Thus he could note the times of arrivals and departures of staff. One night one of his agents, Loris Gheradi, opened the safe, carefully noted exactly how all the documents were placed, and removed what was known as the Black Code. This was hurriedly taken by car to be photographed and was afterwards replaced. There is an alternative version of what happened, that a girl, Bianca Bergami, managed to borrow the code,[21] but this is doubted by Amé.

This particular feat was to prove most productive during a phase in the fighting in North Africa. The Italians did not give the key of this code to the Germans but passed them the decoded texts of signals. As, however, the Germans had an interception station at Lauf, a small town near Nuremberg,[22] they passed signals to Berlin for decoding; there they were soon able, with the assistance of the decoded text, to put together a "shadow" key of their own,* very much as B-Dienst had done with one of our naval systems which was of a similar type, with five-figure groups of numerals as the encoded equivalent of words to which further numerals were added. We are told that it took about two hours to strip off

* Another version is that Rommel's own intelligence unit was equipped with interception apparatus and that decipherment was done by it.[23]

the additional numerals, though this must have depended on the amount of the encoded text.

The signals were of particular value to the enemy, because this system was used by the American Military Attaché in Cairo, Colonel (later General) Bonner Fellers, who was so wordy that he earned the nickname of "Garrulous".[24] He sent a stream of signals to Washington, advising them not only of what had taken place and details of our arms, armour, aircraft and dispositions, but even sent information of what we were *about* to do. As a result Rommel was kept posted with timely information and, able to anticipate our moves, acquired his nickname of "the Desert Fox". Though he was the principal beneficiary of this knowledge, he was not the only one. Thus, when Kesselring was shown an intercept of one of Feller's signals, revealing that British motorized forces had crowded into a *wadi* and got themselves into a traffic jam, he despatched his bombers to attack the closely packed formations.[25]

Similarly, the enemy obtained advance warning of a plan to attack an Axis airfield with the use of both bombs and paratroops; the bombs fell on an empty field and the paratroops were picked off as they landed; casualties were heavy.[26]

On the other hand, Auchinleck who was then quite inadequately equipped to launch a major offensive, used his Ultra advice to outwit Rommel and turn him back when the Germans were at the gates of Cairo.

Later Rommel's own intelligence unit which had received the signals from Lauf was overrun by the Australians and Captain Seebohm, the head of the unit, was killed. More decisively, with the recall to Washington of Fellers, the American system was changed. Simultaneously Rommel's magic touch deserted him.

Amé was a great believer in concentrating his agents on securing the keys of signal systems, for the information which they provided was the latest, most accurate and most reliable. An agent submitting information of a different kind might occasionally strike a plum but often such advice was of limited value and short-lived and could even be a plant. Moreover, times were changing. The days when Bismarck had 40,000 spies in France to "ready the ground" for him belonged to conditions that had become merely historical. But a key to a cipher or code was not only the best and safest source of information but continued to be of value as long as the system remained in use. Keys to embassies and their safes opened many doors. The success attending Amé's policy is undoubted; though in his diary Ciano does not affect to record a complete catalogue of systems read by Italian Intelligence, he mentions them on eleven separate occasions.[27]

However, the Italians were not the only ones to have success in this field of activity, nor were keys to embassy safes always necessary to get results. Early in the war our man in Riga, the capital of the then neutral and independent Latvia, got a tip from a contact who in turn had got it from an agent of the Abwehr, that the Germans were using an illustrated weekly magazine as a means of passing the changes of keys to agents. Each issue carried a crossword puzzle on the cover and from this the key for the following week could be ascertained. A problem which often arises in arranging frequent changes of key is how to get them to users without risk in transit; and this system no doubt appealed to the Germans as a simple and ingenious way out of that difficulty. The British agent in Riga sent a copy of this magazine to his superiors; there was no difficulty about doing that. Our cryptanalysts at Bletchley Park soon worked out the key and thereafter it was merely a matter of studying each weekly issue.[28] Thus the hand ciphers used by the Abwehr were read by us regularly from early 1940; later they changed to machine ciphers which our cryptanalysts read from 1942.[29]

This same agent performed a comparable service and indeed an even more valuable one early in 1943. One of his contacts supplied a clue which in turn enabled Naval Intelligence to break a cipher which had been troubling them for some time. The question naturally leaps to mind: was this one of the major changes to Enigma, mentioned on page 58. It could well have been, for the timing certainly fits. (It might, however, have been Mark II of the bronze goddess which began working some time in 1943.) The clue came from waste paper carelessly thrown out by a German consular official and passed to our agent. He packed off these contents in "the bag" (the courier's pouch); amongst the various pieces of paper, torn or crumpled up, was one piece on which an enciphered telegram had been deciphered. A mistake in the official's working provided the clue which led to the solution.[30]

Diplomatic staff are – or were – notoriously lax about disposing of confidential waste, not bothering about having it destroyed in an incinerator. Many years before precisely the same carelessness in disposing of waste, also by a German diplomatic official, provided the cipher clue that in turn led to the disclosure that Dreyfus had been wrongly convicted.[31] This set an example which has since been followed by agents, often with excellent results, thanks to the carelessness of diplomatic and sometimes military staff. The persistent sifting of waste paper is well-established practice, even if patience is needed before a gratifying result is obtained. Thus, the Russians at one time employed a couple, George and Joanna Wilmer, whose sole task in Tokyo was to photograph the contents of a waste-paper basket of a general on the Imperial General Staff; after they had been doing this for two years, they heard from Moscow that one document photographed had been so valuable that it made up for all the time and expense of the operation since its inception.[32] (This pair of agents incidentally are the same couple who came into the story of the Swiss network.)

In Washington, however, it was the other way round when Hans Thomsen penetrated the State Department's code room, enabling him to obtain access to some of America's top secrets. According to one historian, the head of this department was lax about security.[33] Most, and perhaps even all, of the department's ciphers were thereby compromised. Some of the documents so involved had come from Joseph Kennedy, America's Ambassador in London.

It was this same Thomsen who discovered that the Americans had unravelled the Japanese cipher, Purple. He passed on the tip to Berlin. Whereas the Germans sensibly tightened up their own security in dealing with Baron Oshima, the Japanese Ambassador in Berlin to whom they passed on the tip, the Japanese themselves were so confident that nobody could break their most prized cipher that they then did nothing and continued to use it.[34] The unshakeable faith of the Japanese in their cipher systems was the more remarkable because the *Chicago Tribune* published the fact that Japanese ciphers had been broken.[35] Roosevelt was naturally furious about the disclosure.

Entry by espionage agents to photograph ciphers can, however, have unfortunate results, if they leave any suggestion that the security of ciphers has been compromised. In 1943 two American agents got into the Japanese Embassy in Lisbon and photographed the cipher. It is believed that they did not leave things exactly as they found them. The cipher was changed. The agents did not know that the Americans already knew the key to that particular cipher and unhappily the one which replaced it remained unbroken more than a year later.

Prior to Pearl Harbour, the Japanese are credited with having been the beneficiaries. In 1939 a sixteen-year-old girl, Ruth Kuehn, a mistress of Goebbels, moved with her family to Honolulu where she obtained a post on the staff of a beauty parlour. Recruited to do espionage work for the Japanese, she transmitted encoded information from an attic window to a Japanese agent only five days before the attack on the American Pacific Fleet. The Japanese Consul in Honolulu visited Pearl Harbour and checked the exact position of the American warships. Immediately after the attack the girl and the Japanese agent signalled a report of its success but, while they were doing so, American Intelligence officers burst into the room and arrested them.[36]

Donovan's OSS provided excellent service, notably at the time of the Torch landing in North West Africa. A native fisherman kept the Americans posted about movements of U-boats in the neighbourhood of the Straits of Gibraltar and the coast nearby, and two OSS agents who had secured posts as code clerks in the Spanish Consulate at Rabat provided decoded texts of all German signals passing through the office, while another at Casablanca airport reported Axis arrivals and departures; in addition plans of all airfields, their defences, safety channels and code recognition names were also supplied.[37] Fuller information there could not have been.

Considering the scale of Torch, involving about 550 ships, many of them to pass through the Straits of Gibraltar, plus 1,000 aircraft, it is extraordinary that the enemy were so taken by surprise. The invasion had already been postponed from 30th October on account of security risk. One scare was that there had been reinforcement of the German Air Force in the South of France; this, however, was found to be false.* Another, however, was more worrying. An aircraft carrying a British messenger with plans of the invasion was shot down off the coast of Spain; the man's body was recovered and his papers were passed to the British Consul, apparently untouched.[39] It is, however, difficult to believe that the Spanish authorities did not look at the papers and pass warning to the Germans; they certainly did so when later we arranged for the body of a dead man to be placed in the sea with bogus papers which we wanted passed on to the enemy. On this occasion, however, though we may presume that the papers were read, we must also assume that copies were not passed to Berlin. It seems, therefore, that Canaris, the head of Abwehr, knew of the forthcoming Torch landing. We are even told that he had a complete plan of the invasion,[40] and that he did indeed have ample warning of the gathering of the huge Allied fleet.[41] Our conclusion, therefore, is that Canaris knew what was taking place but deliberately held his peace. In fact he was not the only one of the senior Abwehr officers to turn against Hitler, for Colonel (later Major-General) Oster, one of his closest colleagues, is said to have regularly passed copies of German strategic plans to the Allied intelligence services and, for good measure, to the Vatican as well.[42]

It is known that a revised edition of a tactical code was brought into use for Torch and there seems no doubt that it was not broken by any of the enemy's cipher services.[43] In fact it cannot have been, for two reasons: first, if it had been,

---

* It had been established practice for the GAF to have servicing and repairs for aircraft carried out in the centre of France where they were unlikely to be attacked. Numbers of aircraft varied. It happened that shortly before the original date set for Torch there was a considerable increase; however, information was that the crews had left, mostly for Greece, and that there was no cause for alarm.[38]

enemy intercepts would have kept Berlin posted without any help from Canaris, and, second, the U-boats in that area would not have spent their time going after a routine North-bound convoy.[44] As this was a tactical code, it would not have given the enemy much time, even if he had broken it. What is evident is that when the armada was seen, the enemy could not establish its destination and was taken completely by surprise, Canaris and one or two of his aides excepted, for the fleet passing through the Straits of Gibraltar proceeded beyond the landing beaches,* purposely to mislead, and then turned back.[46]

One wonders what all the espionage agents were doing and what they thought of it, as an almost endless stream of warships and troop carriers made their way through the narrow straits. Casablanca, where some of the American contingent landed, was honeycombed with spies, Allied, German and other agents sitting at adjoining tables at the pavement cafés. In the Kasbah in Tunis numbers of SOE agents were welcomed at a brothel kept by a madame who evidently knew which side to support and was said to have some rare and talented performers[47] who were, in their own way, engaged in the service of the Allies. It need hardly be added that the enemy had innumerable agents in the West Mediterranean.[48] Between them, they must have had an interesting time.

The one man who unquestionably failed to deliver the goods was Canaris. It has been said that he was inefficient. That may be so, but it could be an over-simplification about a man of divided loyalties, and it is possible that some of what has the appearance of inefficiency was deliberately contrived. It might be more accurate to conclude that he was purposely ineffective in his job. Leverkuehn, head of the Abwehr in Turkey, refers to Canaris' rather casual way of initiating new activities[49] but says that he took a lot of care in selecting his staff and that he was rich in intuition.[50]

Canaris was to pay for his failure to serve the Nazi régime faithfully, but it speaks well for the regard in which he was

* Commander Thomas Woodroofe makes the interesting point that this was the first time in history that military expeditions from two different continents landed simultaneously on a third.[45]

Japanese aircraft attack U.S. warships at Ford Island, Pearl Harbour, when much of the American Pacific Fleet was destroyed. The Americans were reading Japanese signals but no timely declaration of war was made.

The Allied Fleet en route to North Africa 'Operation Torch' in action against enemy aircraft. Allied signals were not then read by the Germans who were taken by surprise.

held by his staff, numbering in all about 16,000, that when he was arrested in 1944 and Schellenberg, Heydrich's toady, took over, many felt that they owed their former chief a personal loyalty; at all events they showed what they thought of the change by lack of co-operation, and in Istanbul five of them turned over to the side of the Allies.[51]

One curious point about Canaris' behaviour is why he remained in post until his dismissal and recall to Berlin. If he knew in advance, as he almost certainly did, the objectives of Torch and saw the scale of operations, he cannot have supposed that such a failure to warn Hitler would be overlooked or have doubted that it would bring about his downfall and probably his execution. He was far from *persona grata* with either Heydrich or Himmler. On the other hand he was on excellent terms with Franco who liked him. Yet he made no effort to seek sanctuary in Spain. Perhaps he had a dash of the fatalist in him. He was a curious character and, according to Schellenberg, was in tears at Heydrich's funeral. His must have been the only tears shed for the passing of that apothecary of cruelty.

So far as ciphers and codes were concerned, we can safely conclude that in the Allied landings on Casablanca and principally on the French North African coast, espionage helped to keep the Allies posted with what they needed to know, whereas enemy forces were caught unawares.

*   *   *   *

The most remarkable exploit by an espionage agent feeding information to the enemy and compromising ciphers was that usually known as "Operation Cicero". This took place during the period between September 1943 and April 1944, principally the earlier part of it, at the British Embassy at Ankara.

An Albanian of the name of Elyesa Bazna, calling himself Diello but better known to posterity as Cicero, obtained a post as valet to the Ambassador and, like Toni, had no difficulty getting hold of the keys; he opened the safe, extracted the papers, photographed them, put them back and made a wax impression of the key which he then returned.

On 26th October he called at the German Embassy where he was interviewed by L. C. Moysich who, though posted there, was not a member of the Ambassador's staff, being answerable to Schellenberg. Bazna offered his rolls of film for the sum of £20,000 sterling. Taken aback, Moysich at first refused such a large sum but, when Bazna suggested that, if the German Embassy was not interested, the Russian one would be, Moysich asked for time. Bazna declined to give his name but mentioned his position as the British Ambassador's valet and said that he worked single handed. Moysich consulted von Papen, the German Ambassador, who in turn referred to von Ribbentrop. There was considerable doubt in Berlin whether to accept Bazna's offer as genuine. It was argued that, if he could get access so easily to highly confidential material, the cunning British must have intended him to do so. Among the various intrigues and rivalries that characterized the Nazi régime, however, was the mutual animosity between Kaltenbrunner and von Ribbentrop, and if the latter had his doubts, the influence of Kaltenbrunner evidently prevailed. These doubts were later revived when fingers appeared on one photograph, suggesting that, despite Bazna's assurance that he worked alone, he had an accomplice.[52] However, at the time it was decided to accept the offer, and accordingly the reply was that the deal should be closed. A total of fifty-two negatives were handed over, none of them of documents more than a fortnight old and all of them marked either "Most Secret" or "Top Secret". Bazna was soon in the money, for on 4th November a courier arrived with a suitcase full of Bank of England notes.[53] In December Bazna had a field-day, providing photographed copies of the minutes of the military staff talks held in Teheran during the conference of the Allied leaders. These minutes included mention of the intention to bomb Hungary, Bulgaria and Romania; the first city to be bombed was Sofia and the date set for it was 14th January 1944. The attack took place on the date, removing any lingering doubts whether Bazna's productions were genuine. The minutes of the Cairo conference were also photographed and the rolls of negatives taken to the German Embassy.

In all Bazna was paid about £300,000. Writing in post-war

years, Moysich expressed the view that much of it was counterfeit having been printed in Kaltenbrunner's forgery department,* and he estimated genuine payments to total £40,000. Gehlen did not think any of the money could be counterfeit,[55] but Moysich says that, when the Bank of England later examined some of the notes, they found them to be forgeries.[56]

Since diplomatic ciphers would have been kept in the Embassy safe, the question of their security arises. One view is that Bazna's activities may not have endangered them, as it is known that well before this time radioed signals between London and Ankara were being read.[57] While it does not follow that this was still so at the time of Bazna's activities, Turkish ciphers were not difficult to break; countries with limited budgets could afford little in the way of courier services; accordingly changes of ciphers were difficult to put into effect. Thus it is probable that the Germans were continuing to read Turkish signals. Their texts could have provided tin-openers with which to open ours, particularly if they had quoted extracts from ours, as is quite commonly done in diplomatic communications. Schellenberg, however, tells us that near the end of 1943 General Thiele was instructed to tackle the diplomatic system, that he engaged the services of the four most talented specialists in Germany, two of them professors of mathematics at universities, and that they were finally able to unravel part of the system which he considered a tremendous achievement.[58] Thus, if Schellenberg's version is correct, intensive work on Bazna's material endangered the system. Cadogan of the Foreign Office evidently accepted that this was the case.[59]

It is known that it was through the services of an agent, a German who had secured a post in the German Foreign Office, that Allen Dulles got the tip about Bazna and passed it on to the British Embassy.[60]

*   *   *   *

* This department's work is believed to have been extremely thorough. According to Schellenberg, it took two years to produce the identical type of paper used for Bank of England notes and then the employment of the most skilful engravers[54]; £10,000,000 of notes were dumped on to the money market in 1943.

British subjects who turned against their own country, working for other countries, fall into two categories. There must have been very few who went over to the Germans; one of them whose identity is public knowledge was William Joyce who was not, however, a spy but broadcast to Britain for Germany during the war and acquired the nickname of Lord Haw-haw. Even in his case there is a qualification, for the defence of Joyce at his trial after the war was that he had renounced his British nationality and had become a German subject. Whether the renunciation was enough was the question; the court decided that it was ineffective and he was hanged.

In a quite different category there were three men who, as afterwards became known, were agents for Russia; these were H. A. R. (Kim) Philby, Guy Burgess and Donald McLean. As Russia was one of our Allies during much of the war, these men were as much anti-Hitler as anyone else and in that sense, therefore, there appeared to be nothing against them. Their careers extended into post-war years with which we are not concerned, but the war-time years of two of them come into our story.

Philby's father who had been in the Indian Civil Service had been a pretty unpleasant man and it is not surprising that the son was too, though he lacked the obvious aggressiveness of his father. John le Carré, a master of the use of words, has summed him up in a few pungent sentences. "Deceit was his life, deceit, as I understand it, his nature ... Philby has no home, no woman, no faith ... the self-hate of a vain mis-fit ... the little man who found a big name for cheating."[61] Burgess in a different way was hardly less undesirable. He has been described as "indirect, drunken and unreliable"[62] to which might be added that he was aggressively homosexual. Yet both these had managed to impress persons in authority and even secured appointments in our secret services, and both did contribute certain services of note involving revelations of espionage and the use of ciphers.

Philby had been working for the Russians before the outbreak of war,[63] when he became correspondent of *The Times*. He had been recommended by Sir Joseph Ball to

Admiral Sir Hugh Sinclair, then head of MI6, whose death unfortunately occurred when the war was barely three months old. Sinclair who was an exceptionally astute judge of character, took an immediate dislike to Philby and would have nothing to do with him.[64]

Such unusually shrewd judgement of character is a particularly important attribute for senior men in secret services – and, for that matter, for agents who have to choose their contacts. Ball who had been a MI5 man was not possessed of it; indeed he himself has been described as "a shadowy character".[65] The head of MI5 on the outbreak of war was Major-General Sir Vernon Kell who, on the contrary, had an extraordinary and distinguished career, having held that post since 1909 when it was known as MO5, later as Special Intelligence. His term of office was to last for thirty-one years, a record likely to stand for all time. Though criticisms have been made of Kell, he made few mistakes and he built up an outstanding organization which served the country wonderfully well in both world wars. But his best days were behind him by 1939.

Disastrously for Kell two unfortunate circumstances occurred early in the war. The first happened on 14th October 1939 when the *Royal Oak* was torpedoed and sunk by a U-boat in Scapa Flow with the loss of 834 lives,* and the second on 18th January 1940 when three bombs exploded in the Royal Ordnance gunpowder factory at Waltham Abbey, notwithstanding that a guard had been mounted by Special Branch detectives after consultation with MI5, which took the rap for both these occasions. Kell was called upon by Churchill to resign; he was then sixty-seven and died two years later. Pending the appointment of Sir David Petrie as his successor, temporary arrangements were made. Thus in the early stages of the war there were changes at the top, as

* After the First World War a German named von Scheillermann came to this country where he settled and in 1932 became a naturalized British subject. He made his home in Kirkwall where he ran a jeweller's shop. He was, or possibly later became, a German agent and in 1939 he advised his superiors in Berlin that the Eastern approaches to Scapa Flow had not been closed by mines. It is believed that after passing this information he left Kirkwall for Leith where he took a ship to Rotterdam and so escaped.[66]

well as in less senior posts, in both MI5 and SIS. But it is not quite fair to cast all the blame on to these services for allowing characters such as Philby and Burgess to secure appointments with SIS. Indeed in 1938 Burgess who had visited Chartwell, Westerham, had so impressed Churchill that he was presented with an inscribed copy of Churchill's speeches entitled *Arms and the Covenant.* Ball was a supporter not only of Philby but of Burgess as well and, when Kell left, Ball exercised a certain amount of influence.

In fact both these two performed services which were all that could have been expected of them, and it is with these that we are concerned.

Early in the war Churchill entered into frequent communications with Roosevelt; they were to continue throughout the war. During the initial period they were written and were taken by courier to the United States Embassy where they were handed to the Ambassador, Joseph Kennedy. They were then encoded in a system believed to be unbreakable. Of some of these communications the contents were believed to be known to nobody in this country other than Churchill, Ambassador Kennedy and his code clerk, and to nobody in America other than Roosevelt and his code clerk.

Meantime our own cryptanalysts, employed at the Government Codes and Cipher School at Bletchley Park were getting on with their job of reading enemy signals that had been intercepted and passed to them. In the course of reading signals passing between Hans Mackensen, the German Ambassador in Rome, and the German Foreign Office, it came to light that the contents of some of these highly confidential exchanges between Churchill and Roosevelt were known to the enemy and had no doubt been passed by von Ribbentrop to Hitler. After the war it was disclosed that the number of these secret communications known to Berlin was about 1,500.[67] Since the war was then in its early stages, only just out of what was known as the phoney war, the number of these communications is rather remarkable and suggests that there was not much of importance that the two leaders did not share.

How these exchanges came to be known to the enemy

would have remained a mystery for longer but for the action of an Italian journalist named Luigi Barzini, the son of the editor of an Italian newspaper published in New York and firmly anti-Fascist. It was he who gave the tip that one of the Allied top ciphers was being read.[68] The Italians had got an espionage agent operating within the British Embassy itself. In fact this dated back to 1935 when one Francesco Constantini, then on the staff, regularly removed the contents of the waste-paper baskets; this included copies of diplomatic correspondence, both cabled and carried by courier. He also had access to ciphers in the safe; he it was who sold copies of his discoveries to the Russian Embassy and was emboldened to steal the diamond tiara belonging to the wife of the British Ambassador. There were no flies on Constantini who retired in 1937, no doubt by then comfortably off, but passed on – or perhaps sold – the tip to his successor.[69] It was through the usual documents lifted from the Embassy that Barzini's secret advice to the Embassy was betrayed.[70] One might think that, considering the risk Barzini was taking and the value of his services, the Embassy staff might have taken the trouble to protect his secret which should never have been recorded in writing.

The action of Barzini who was a doughty character thus became known to the Italians and he was arrested. He was sent to an island prison where no doubt he congratulated himself on his good fortune in not being executed. What exactly Barzini disclosed to the Embassy beyond the bare fact stated has not been made public but, as a result of his information, it became evident that the leak originated in the United States Embassy in London.

The man who completed the tip-off was none other than Guy Burgess; his action was so much appreciated that he was afterwards invited to spend a week-end at Chequers as the guest of the Prime Minister.

There was in London a former Czarist Admiral Wolkov who had been Naval Attaché in the last Imperial Russian Embassy. Between the wars he and his wife opened a Russian tea room, at 50 Harrington Gardens, South Kensington. On account of his known sympathies with the Hitler régime he was interned by Sir John Anderson (later Lord Waverley) during the Second World War and spent his time in the Isle of Man. He had a daughter, Anna, who was strongly and openly anti-Jewish. She would go about at night sticking up notices on walls to the effect that the war was the doing of the Jews. Though this activity was known, she was for a time thought to be no more than a harmless nuisance. In fact she turned out to be considerably more than that. She was never an espionage agent in the sense of being formally a member of the enemy's secret service, but her strong anti-Jewish convictions led her to throw in her hand with the Nazi régime.

Anna Wolkov was thirty-eight when war broke out. She made common cause with Tyler Kent, a twenty-three-year-old cipher clerk employed at the American Embassy who, early in 1939, had been posted to Moscow and in October of that year was transferred to London. She was a woman of some attractions, and it was from him that she obtained information about the Churchill-Roosevelt communications. They decided to entrust the work of photographing these documents to a commercial photographer who, without being aware of what was afoot, undertook to do the job. The full story of what followed has not been disclosed, but it is said that the Duke of Del Monte who was a frequent visitor to the tea rooms, and also an acquaintance of Anna Wolkov at either the Romanian or the Italian Embassy, acted as her channels of communication. She was in frequent touch by letter with William Joyce.[71] Both she and Tyler Kent were unaware that they were being watched. A visit was paid by detectives to the photographer who willingly produced documents of which he had been asked to make copies.[72] Though they were marked "most secret" he had not tumbled to what was afoot.

The American Ambassador, Joseph Kennedy, was shaken by the disclosures. Kent was dismissed and, immediately losing his diplomatic immunity, was arrested by Special Branch detectives who were waiting outside the Embassy. He and Anna Wolkov were tried *in camera* when Kent was abusive and arrogant. He was sentenced to seven years' imprisonment; he was released in 1945 and deported. Anna Wolkov was sentenced to ten years; she served her sentence

in Aylesbury prison and was released in June 1946 after five
and a half years. She was deprived of her British nationality
which she had acquired through naturalization papers and
was required to leave the country. She went to the Continent
and settled in France where she lived till 1972 when she died
following injuries received in a motor crash.

As for Burgess, he later fled to Russia where he drank
himself to death.

This was the most important but not the only help to find
enemy agents or sources of information leaving this country,
provided by Burgess or his colleagues. For Philby came into
contact with an attaché at the Portuguese Embassy in London. The full names of this young man, then twenty-six years
old, were Rogerio de Magalhas Peixoto de Menezes, who
had been posted to London in July 1942. His salary was then
twenty-five pounds per month which, even then, allowed
only a reasonably modest scale of living. What first attracted
Philby's attention to him was the lavish spending of this
exceptionally hospitable young man who certainly did not
seem short of funds. Why was he so hospitable? Was he being
paid by somebody and, if so, by whom? His suspicions
aroused, Philby mentioned his name and suggested that his
activities might be worth watching. They were, for de
Menezes was busy trying to secure certain information: the
location of London's anti-aircraft defences, the food situation
in Britain and also the production of war material. He was
given to writing long letters and arrangements were made to
open them and have a look at them. Cipher specialists had
little difficulty unravelling the cipher he used, for it was a
simple one. The invisible ink with which he wrote between
the well spaced lines and in the margins was of poor
quality.[73] What this correspondence revealed was not on the
level of the espionage work carried out by Anna Wolkov and
Tyler Kent, but it was serious enough. The Ambassador was
advised and dismissed de Menezes who was arrested as he
left the Embassy. Philby's alert observations about this
young man undoubtedly stood him in good stead.

Philby must have been thought a useful and trustworthy
character, for on another occasion he was entrusted with an
investigation, also involving Portugal. The Abwehr were

understood to have a ring in Lisbon known as Ostro, the head of it being one Fidrmuc, who was believed to employ three agents referred to as Ostro 1, Ostro 2 and Ostro 3. In fact these were what was called "notional", that is, non-existent, used by Fidrmuc as a means of bilking the Abwehr of funds.[74]

*   *   *   *

On both sides it was the practice to turn spies where opportunity served, that is, to engage them to work against their own country by transmitting information which it was intended that the enemy should accept as genuine. Thus the Germans turned Russian agents whom they caught to work for Germany.[75] There was nothing new in this, but in the Second World War the practice was developed on a scale not previously approached, and the country that was most successful doing this was Britain. The story of our success in so doing has been the subject of a separate book[76] and it is sufficient here to sketch how this was done. In effect we operated and effectively controlled the Abwehr espionage system* in this country.

J. C. (later Sir John) Masterman was the head of the XX Committee, sometimes referred to as the Twenty Committee or Double-cross Committee, on which the three Armed Services, the Foreign Office and the Ministry of Home Security were represented.

Apart from the fact that these operations contributed to our familiarity with the enemy's ciphers, it was unlikely that a particular system would be changed, because of the difficulties which would have arisen with agents in this country. Each agent who was turned was continuously looked after and controlled by a "case officer" who knew the man's case intimately and maintained detailed records. Building up agents in this way was protracted and laborious. Clearly the XX Committee could not finance the agents without giving things away, and some agents were short of

---

* The Abwehr was divided into four sections. One was general administration, a second was concerned with active espionage, a third with sabotage, and a fourth with counter-espionage and security.

money; one indeed committed suicide because of lack of funds.[77]

Agents would make visits to factories on which they had been ordered to report, so that what they reported met the demands of credibility, whether concerning troop movements, arms production, coastal defences or anything else.[78] An example of the practical effect of these reports is one about bogus minefields which resulted in closing an area of sea of about 3,600 square miles.[79]

Through contacts with the Abwehr the position was reached where the identity of new agents was known before they had arrived.[80] Not all the agents were Germans. Some were Yugoslavs who joined the Abwehr in order to cross to this country and become double agents working for the Allies. One of the outstanding of these was Dusko Popov who built up a *coterie* of double agents.

One of the most important functions of the double-agent system was what was referred to as "Operation Starkey", the feeding to the enemy of false information about the Second Front.[81] Supporting this was a series of false signals and the creation of notional armies with dummy tanks and barges in the Dover area ("Operation Fortitude"). A great deal of detailed planning was involved to maintain credibility and see that it all fitted together. There was even a false Field Marshal Montgomery, the actor M. E. Clifton-Jones, impersonating him with medals and all.[82] How successful this ruse was is demonstrated by the fact that the enemy was so confident that the main invading force would be directed at the Pas de Calais area that a fortnight after the landing Jodl still had fifteen divisions in the region of Calais.

Probably half, and perhaps a little more, of the total number of enemy agents in Britain were controlled in this way, enciphering and transmitting to their superiors the information which the Allies wanted transmitted. It should also be recorded that MI5 got excellent help from the GPO whose direction-finding vans were constantly on the prowl, monitoring the various transmissions. (Radios in private cars were forbidden, whether installed or portable.)

Most of the agents selected by the enemy for recruitment were no doubt men with a natural inclination to concealment and intrigue and were probably not fussy about which side they spied for. The Germans are believed to have released from prison certain criminals who, in return for remission of their sentences, undertook to engage in espionage activities. One of those who volunteered and was accepted was landed in this country. He immediately found his way to the nearest police station where he announced that he was a German spy. As, however, he had not indulged in any espionage activities, he could not be charged with doing so, and the problem arose of what to do with him. It was believed that reasons could be found to detain him pending His Majesty's pleasure which would have meant interning him till the end of the war.[83] But whether this course was taken lies in some dusty file buried in the secret archives.

NINE

THE BAKER STREET IRREGULARS
Special Operations Executive

On a small house at 1 Dorset Square by Baker Street, London, there is a plaque bearing the following inscription:

> This plaque is erected to commemorate
> the deeds of men and women of the
> Free French Forces
> and their British comrades
> who left from this house on special missions
> to enemy-occupied France
> and to honour those who did not return
> 1941-1944

It stands as a memorial to a body officially named in characteristically Civil Service style "Special Operations Executive" (SOE) and, with a touch of Sherlock Holmes, unofficially known as the "Baker Street Irregulars". The house is one of a number in this neighbourhood used as their London headquarters.

Fundamentally this body differed from the three armed forces in that no comparable established staff college existed with knowledge and experience of irregular warfare. In the words of Colonel Buckmaster, one of the senior officers on the administration: "It was no use trying to do things by the book – there was no book."[1]

Nor unfortunately can it be said that they got willing help from the Chiefs of Staff whose attitude towards them varied between being merely unhelpful to being downright hostile. The conventional and orthodox minds of the Service Chiefs were not adjusted to irregular warfare; to them the Baker

Street Irregulars were amateurs and upstarts who did not fit into their conception of how warfare should be conducted.

As an official historian, Sir James Butler remarks, these doubts were embittered by personal animosities.[2] The responsible Minister may not have been the easiest of men to get on with and at times he was explosive, but considering what he had to put up with, he had something to explode about, for the Chiefs of Staff were not the only ones to show hostility. Oliver Lyttleton (later Lord Chandos) complained of "chaos ... lack of security, waste of public funds and ineffectiveness of SOE ... deplorable conditions ... of which I had incontestable proof".[3] If SOE's actual enemies were confined to foreign lands, they certainly had some remarkably unfriendly people in their own country.

The hostility to irregular warfare was not confined to SOE, for Combined Operations suffered from the same prejudice; it took the imaginative mind of Mountbatten to appreciate the possibilities of something which was quite new. It was as well that we had his immense services at our disposal and not only for the contribution forthcoming from Combined Operations.*

A more adaptable attitude than that of the orthodox Chiefs of Staff was that of SIS where there is also no book,[5] and it was in one of their sections, in a country house near Hatfield, that in 1938 thought was given to devising methods of irregular warfare, training in industrial sabotage and other subversive activities.[6]

It may be said that SOE's date of birth was 19th July 1940. The minister responsible for it initially was Hugh (later Lord) Dalton who, some time after it was a going concern, was succeeded by Lord Selborne. Dalton's position was not made any easier by the fact that he was not a member of the War Cabinet; but he was an individualist with an independent mind and plenty of determination. He needed both those qualities in the task assigned to him.

Dalton divided SOE into two branches, SO1 and SO2. The former was concerned with propaganda to enemy-

---

* It was he who insisted that the Second Front should not be directed at the Pas de Calais area which was favoured by a number of Generals and Air Marshals and was where the enemy expected it.[4]

occupied territories and was later renamed Political Warfare Executive (PWE). SO2 was concerned with operations, and it is to this branch that we direct our attention.

The man in charge of military action was Brigadier (later Major-General Sir) Colin Gubbins. The scope geographically was so wide that it included France, Belgium, Holland, Norway, Denmark, Poland, Austria, Czechoslovakia, Yugoslavia, Greece, Cyprus, Crete, West Africa, Tunis, the Middle East, the Dodecanese islands, Romania, Bulgaria, and even India, Ceylon and Japan, though it was in France that it was operated on the largest scale. In certain areas it failed to achieve very much; in Greece it hardly got off the ground and was a wasted effort.[7]

Training schools were set up, each specializing in a particular country, and agents had to undergo a course of preparation. They were carefully watched, in particular their drinking habits and whether they talked in their sleep. They underwent commando training and in Scotland took a course of practice over wild, mountainous country, learning how to hide from patrols, hand-to-hand combat, judo and so on. They were taught the use of explosives and how to sabotage German aircraft of which a number were available for use, how to attach explosives to trains, using engines and rolling stock provided by railway companies, the construction of tank traps, how to defuse mines, and the use of poisons. They learnt parachute jumping at Ringway Airport, Manchester and elsewhere. They attended courses about the military and police organizations in Germany and the occupied territories; and they were provided with identity cards, work permits and residence permits, stamped with replicas of the official rubber stamps made from specimens obtained through secret agents. A tailor who specialized in continental fashions provided clothes of the type used in other countries. Equipment included infra-red torches, little maps of localities rolled up in the shaft of propelling pencils, miniature compasses hidden in cuff links and bootlaces in which were hidden gigi saws* for wire-cutting, and suitcases of foreign design.[8]

There was much to be admired in the thoroughness and

* Gigi saws are used in brain surgery.

imagination shown in the detailed preparations and training of SOE agents.

The frosty attitude of the Chiefs of Staff was by no means the only trouble between SOE and others. Indeed a much more difficult one, virtually intractable in one case, was the relationship with the exiled governments and national committees in this country. This was probably inevitable, for Churchill himself had definite ideas about the roles and operations of SOE agents, and these often conflicted with those of exiled leaders who were naturally concerned about the reprisals which sometimes followed these activities. Thus in Norway the patriotic resistance movement was the Milorg; relations between this body and SOE became so strained that by the end of 1941 co-operation between them had practically come to a standstill. SOE agents themselves were of course aware of this, and in November of that year sixteen men who had been sent to Norway, having escaped from a glider that crashed, declined to imperil the lives of civilians by accepting their assistance to escape and instead surrendered to the Germans. They were tortured and executed.*

The difficult personal relations between de Gaulle and British war leaders inevitably spilt over into these operations and, for a period at least, de Gaulle forbade any contact between his Secret Service officers and the staff of SOE. Even if Giraud had been recognized as France's leader, as the Americans would have preferred, difficulties would no doubt still have arisen.

It was naturally in France that most of the operations were carried out, but by no means all those who combined together in resistance to the enemy formally joined the *Armée Secrète*, the para-military organization, any more than all those in Holland joined the Orde Dienst, the corresponding body. Various other groups were formed of which the Maquis became the best known. Their aims were summed up in three words, *surprise, mitraillade, évanouissement,* which may be translated as "surprise, shoot, vanish". Their hatred of the Nazis was surpassed only by their hostility

---

* After the war their bodies were recovered and buried with military honours in Egenes graveyard in Stavanger.

Leopold Trepper, the head of Rote Kapelle and probably Russia's ablest espionage agent who three times sent advance warnings to Stalin of the German attack on Russia.

A long-range rocket captured in Germany. These and flying bombs were together intended to be released at about one thousand a day, enough to require the evacuation of London. But on advance warnings signalled by agents the base at Peenemunde was heavily bombed.

The artificially constructed Mulberry Harbour, transported to Normandy and supplemented by pipe lines under the Channel carrying fuel supplies. The use of bogus signals by captured German agents, directed by MI5, contributed much to misleading the Germans about the assault area.

towards the *milice*, Vichy French sympathizers who collaborated with the Gestapo.[10] The womenfolk of the Maquis were no less intrepid than the men. One of them stood at a road junction during German troop movements after the opening of the Second Front and directed an enemy battalion into an Allies' trap. The American war correspondent, Virginia Hall, who had a wooden leg, was nonetheless a woman of great endurance and spirit and guided agents and sometimes supplied them with funds. She worked for SOE and extended her help to any resistance workers.

Another of the remarkable woman agents from other countries was the Countess Skarbeck, better known as Christine Granville who was a girl when war broke out and married to a Pole considerably older than herself. They were then in Abyssinia.[11] She applied to join our SIS and went to Budapest and into Poland. Her activities extended to smuggling out Poles and other Allied officers. She had many narrow escapes and in 1942, when she was in Cairo, she became the first woman parachutist in the Middle East and in that year was dropped to the Vercors Plateau in the Rhone Valley where she joined the Maquis leader, Colonel François Cammaerts. In 1944 three Panzer divisions were sent to deal with the Maquis. On two occasions she was caught but made nimble escapes and on the third occasion claimed to be the niece of Field Marshal Montgomery and was released. She was awarded the GC and the OBE after the war and settled in London where in 1952 she was murdered. (Her murder had nothing to do with her wartime activities.)

In their fight against the Germans the Maquis showed superb heroism. Those on the Plateau des Glières were the first to fight a pitched battle with the enemy – 450 men against 10,000 men of the German Mountain Division.[12] In their service, radioing encoded messages, the BBC served the Maquis as well as SOE agents. Unfortunately for the Maquis their own ciphers were not difficult to unravel and the Germans read them as easily as we did.[13]

The administration of SOE had first to determine if there was a resistance movement in each of the various occupied territories, then arrange communications of intelligence, then transport of agents, and finally the supply of equipment and arms.

The first presented obvious risks, in particular enemy agents posing as local patriots, but exiled governments and national committees provided much valuable help and advice, and in the event there proved to be such movements throughout the whole of occupied Western Europe, Poland and other countries. Thus was to be demonstrated the truth that no man can antagonize the whole world without being overtaken by nemesis.

Communications of intelligence were of first importance, for the system could not have worked otherwise. What was required was a suitable type of wireless receiver-cum-transmitter that was not too heavy and, in its case, resembled ordinary hand luggage. Not all cases should be of the same appearance, or the capture of one agent with one would lead to the arrest on sight of anybody else seen carrying the same type of case. By 1944 it was estimated that there were 150 such wireless sets in France alone.

There were certain sea communications. One was what became known as the "Shetland bus", a ferry service between a point just North of Lerwick and Norway, used both for the transport of men, high explosives and other materials, and for bringing over Norwegian volunteers to this country. There was also a large French submarine of 1,700 tons, the *Casabianca,* which escaped from Toulon the morning the fleet there was sunk; she transported agents under the leadership of a venturesome and enterprising Commander L'herminier.[14] She was so large that on one occasion she was used to transport an entire company of French infantry. Agents being landed from the sea wore gas capes (afterwards taken back by the crew) over their clothes to prevent them being stained by any tell-tale marks of sea spray.* No headgear was

---

* Failure to take this precaution resulted in the arrest of two German agents put ashore at Buckpool, Banffshire, in September 1940. When they bought their railway tickets, it was noted that their clothes were wet up to the knees. On reaching Edinburgh one of them put his case in the cloakroom at Waverley Station where the police, alerted, noticed that it bore the white mark of salt spray. The case was opened and found to contain a wireless transmitter. When the agent came to collect it, he was arrested after a struggle with Constable Merrilees (later to

worn lest in the hurry to get away it should fall off and so leave a clue to alert the police.[16] But many agents were transported to France by aircraft; often they were dropped by parachute but, given a suitable landing site, a small light aircraft could touch down and a minute later take off again. Numbers of agents were likewise brought back on visits to this country.

One problem which arose was how to keep agents supplied with money. Large sums would on occasion be dropped by parachute, but a barter arrangement was later made with bankers or others in France. A personal message was suggested by the lender and the agent would then signal it as confirmation of the agent's *bona fides,* the sum to be repaid after the war. (In fact not all those who had lent money in this way asked to be reimbursed when the time came, no doubt deriving satisfaction from having contributed to this gallant enterprise.)

The rule was that if an agent in France chanced to recognize another whom he had met during the course of his training, he should ignore his colleague. Such could occur, for example, in a railway compartment, when the temptation to communicate was strong, for service as an agent was not only highly dangerous but, like most secret service work, lonely, and the urge to snatch a little relaxation with a colleague was hard to resist. About the only circumstance which headquarters recognized as justifying such communication was when advice about escape routes needed to be passed.

During the initial stages when SOE were beginning to get into shape, de Gaulle's own organization, *Bureau Central des Renseignements et d'Action (Militaire)* was established under Captain (later Colonel) Dewavrin (codename "Passy"). Their headquarters in Duke Street were almost destroyed by a bomb in one of the air attacks on London in the spring of 1941. They were then sending their own agents over to France and got away to a flying start. What deeply offended the Free French was that SOE which was essentially a British organization and was independently pursuing the task of

become Chief Constable of the Lothians and Peebles and a notable figure locally). Both agents were executed.[15]

recruiting, training and in time sending their own agents to France and setting up networks there, invited and often received the co-operation of resistance workers. This attitude was inevitable and one can readily understand the resentment felt by de Gaulle and his aides.

It is impossible to say just who did and did not belong to SOE. Many of those who lent a hand in France, sometimes a valuable and always a welcome one, had not been formally recruited. But on the figures available – for what they are worth – in midsummer 1944 which was probably the peak period the number in France might have been as many as 10,000 men and 3,200 women.[17]

*   *   *   *

One of the most remarkable characteristics of SOE was the encoded communications from London. There was nothing hidden about their transmission, for they were broadcast by the BBC. This idea was put forward by an agent named Georges Bégué* in the summer of 1941, and thereafter there were regular transmissions from Bush House in the Strand. These became continuous, day and night, in the various languages required. Use was made of code phrases or sentences for messages of a standard type.

Thus, after the introduction, *Ici Londres. Voici quelques messages personnels,* an instruction might be disguised in such forms as:

> La chienne de Barbara aura trois chiots,
> Romeo embrasse Juliette,
> Esculape n'aime pas le mouton,
> Mieux tard que jamais,
> Et le désir s'accroît quand l'effet se ridicule,

or   Les éléphants mangent les fraises.

For transmissions to this country each agent had his own key, agreed with him before he left Britain, being one that he could readily remember. Each was also to make use of what was known as a security check, as a demonstration that the

---

* Bégué was the first agent to be parachuted into France. The date was the night of 10th March 1941.

message he was sending was genuine and that he had not been captured and was not therefore signalling under duress. The instructions were that, if he had been caught and was required to transmit a signal, he should do so but should omit his security check. London would then know what had happened. The security check was simple enough; it might take the form of a spelling error in, say, the fifth word or in the fourth letter of any word.

Agents were told to pay strict attention to brevity.[18] Nothing should be transmitted at any greater length than necessary. They were told to transmit only when essential, to do so at irregular intervals but at certain scheduled times, on various wave-lengths and from various places. Unfortunately, on occasion an agent who had found a household where he or she was welcomed was tempted to transmit from that house several times, and with direction-finders on the prowl this could be, and usually was, fatal. It was soon found that a transmission of any length from a large town would probably bring a direction-finding van to the door within half an hour.

Sometimes reception from the field was bad and a cryptographer decoding in London could not always tell which mistakes were intended and which were accidental, for transmitting in clandestine conditions, perhaps with frozen fingers, was liable to error. It also had the disadvantage of killing the agent's natural rhythm or "handwriting" of which a copy had been made in London before the agent was sent over.

Unfortunately, the system of security checks was by no means fool-proof. It may be that there were occasions when agents overlooked including their security checks. But unfortunately there were certainly others when they did so deliberately, having been caught, and to their consternation received replies from London saying, "Watch it, old boy. Your mind must be wandering. You left out your security check".[19] One agent who survived a term in Buchenwald afterwards told how he had met others who in similar circumstances had received the same sort of casual response from London, as he asked, "What the hell was the check meant for if it was not for that very special reason?"[20]

Perhaps in the comfort of Baker Street headquarters there was a psychological tendency to overconfidence which was not always alert to recognize that the worst had happened.[21]

After the war there were in some quarters suggestions that sometimes an agent had been deliberately sacrificed. There was, however, no truth whatsoever in this unjustified allegation. Mistakes were made because it was human to err and for no other reason.

Seen against the background of the many thousands of signals sent by agents, such tragic mistakes in London no doubt formed a tiny proportion; Cookridge records that up to 2 million words in all passed through SOE signals in an average week.[22] But that of course could have been no consolation to the unfortunate agents involved. The casualty rate among agents was extremely high, considerably higher than in the merchant marine and far higher than in the armed forces. We are told that the average life-span of an agent in action was no more than three weeks.[23] If that is true, it is surprising that the casualty roll was not even higher than it was. To be dropped in occupied France was to engage in a highly dangerous struggle against a ruthless foe and often the reward was death.

Sometimes the Germans indulged in what was called the "play-back game" when they had captured an agent and continued to signal his headquarters as though he himself were doing so of his own free will. One of these agents named Gilbert Norman (code name "Archambaud") was required to transmit and, after being playfully rebuked by London for omitting his security check, was executed. Messages continued to be sent to London as from him. Another agent, Gaston Cohen, advised London that Archambaud had been caught; he received the reply: "You must be mistaken because Archambaud is still transmitting to us."

It is not difficult to appreciate that there were problems at headquarters because of conditions which could account for the obliteration of an agent's "handwriting" or, in certain cases, because the agent, after a period of torture, had given away his security check.

One of the problems facing agents was the choice of places from which to transmit their signals. One answer was what became known as "Operation Lavatory".[24] The agent would hide his wireless transmission set in a lavatory cistern of a safe house; there was a specially designed pulling chain to provide an aerial. Codes could be written in invisible ink on underwear. The only disadvantage of this system was the obvious one that the agent, having found a friendly household that he could trust, would be tempted to transmit from it once too often instead of from a variety of points.

Routine messages could, however, be transmitted with the maximum economy which at least served the aims of brevity. The following are extracts from what was known as the "Q code":*

QRB: Your message regarding broadcast received and understood.
QRJ: Nothing heard from you.
QRM: Interference is bad.
QRT: Stop sending.
QRU: I have nothing for you.
QTP: Accept my priority message at once.
QUO: I am forced to stop transmitting owing to imminent danger. If possible, I will try to make contact with you on my next schedule.

Where a routine system would not meet the case, an agent had to use a cipher. In the earlier phases this was sometimes a simple Bigram type, based on a single word. An example is given below.

Let us assume that the key word is "France". The square is worked out with the letters of that word appearing first, the remaining letters being set out in alphabetical order; the

* This type of code was not uncommon. Thus a similar one was found on a German agent arrested by Constable Merrilees in Edinburgh on 30th September 1940.[25]

QRM:	Disturbance in sending.	QSY:	Please change frequency.
QRV:	I am ready.	TMW:	Tomorrow.
QSV:	Will you send a series.	VY:	Indecipherable.
QRX:	Wait till ( ) o'clock.	NW:	Now.

letters I and J share a position, making the square five by five. The product now reads as follows:

F	R	A	N	C
E	B	D	G	H
I/J	K	L	M	O
P	Q	S	T	U
V	W	X	Y	Z

Suppose that the words of the text are "Sites destroyed", we set this out with letters in pairs, as follows:

SI TE SD ES TR OY ED

We now encipher from the table above, two letters at a time. Where a pair appears in the same horizontal line, we use the letters to the right of each; for the letter to the right of the last in the line we use the first. We apply a similar rule vertically when pairs of letters appear in the same vertical column. Where pairs of letters appear in neither the same horizontal line nor the same vertical column, the letters at opposite positions, forming a square or rectangle, are used. So our encipherment appears as follows:

SI TE SD ES TR OY ED
PL PG XL DP QN MZ BG

We now write it out with the letters grouped into fives. As the final group make only four, we complete that five by adding what is called a "null". ("Nulls" are not part of the text and are used merely to fit the method.) Our completed text therefore reads as follows:

PLPGX   LDPQN   MZBGZ

This is known as the Bigram or Playfair cipher and was first constructed before the Boer War. Though it is a simple one, it has the attraction of suppressing letter frequencies. In the example given, the letter E, the most commonly used in English, appears three times in the plain text but in the enciphered text it is represented on the first occasion by G, on the second by D and on the third by B.

A second type of cipher used also involved a tabular key

and was likewise simple to use. Let us assume that the
message which the agent wishes to transmit is "Expect drop
tomorrow night". We also assume that his security check is
a spelling error in the fifth letter of any word and that he
decides to spell the first word "Expept".

He first writes out some jumbled letters of his choice, say
an anagram of his code name "Pithy" which he spells "Hi-
typ" to which he adds his initials, V.B. To these he adds on
the words of his message, completing a checkerboard. Above
each column he enters some jumbled numerals. The product
then looks like this:

4	6	9	1	7	10	2	5	3	8
H	I	T	Y	P	V	B	E	X	P
E	P	T	D	R	O	P	T	O	M
O	R	R	O	W	N	I	G	H	T

The letters are now written out in groups of five, reading
the columns vertically, starting with column 1 and
concluding with column 10. The result is as follows:

YDOBP IXOHH EOETG IPRPR WPMTT TRVON

The recipient, knowing in advance the key letters and the
order of the numbered columns, has no difficulty reading the
message.

Other systems used have not been disclosed, but we know
that the one-time random pad was one; this has already been
explained, but there was one difference in the type of pad
used to that adopted by the Russians. Whereas the latter
used a type of leaf that was destructable both easily and
immediately, the type used by SOE was made of silk slips
and these were not always so easy to destroy.[26] This type of
cryptogram was unquestionably the safest in that it was
unbreakable, but it had the obvious and inevitable disadvantage that anyone found in possession of one was a
condemned man; in that sense a system that could be
memorized was undoubtedly much safer.

It is pleasant to record that Dewavrin, the head of de
Gaulle's Secret Service, held the technical service of SOE in
high regard.[27]

While Dewavrin's high opinion of the British signals service was no doubt justified, so far as SOE operations in most
countries were concerned, there was one frightful exception
that fell far short of the usual standard, so much so that it
became a terrible tragedy. The importance of maintaining
an efficient and alert service was never more dramatically
demonstrated than in the Dutch disaster.

In the early stages of the war relations between the British
and the Dutch services were about as bad as they could have
been, mainly due in the first place to British refusal to allow
the Dutch to have their own transmitters,[28] but eventually
things were worked out with Colonel J. M. Somer, head of
the Dutch Military Intelligence in exile.

The man in charge of the Abwehr in the Netherlands was
Major Hermann Giskes who, fortunately for the Dutch, did
not resort to the use of torture – fortunately for himself,
too, after the war when the War Crimes Commission was
established.

In November 1941 one George Ridderhof, a criminal with
a record of peddling narcotics and other such activities, was
in prison awaiting trial on a charge of smuggling diamonds
into Belgium. While in prison he heard whispers of the Orde
Dienst and of a Captain van der Berg who was a member of
it. Ridderhof offered, in return for his release, to give his
information to the enemy and to help follow it up by acting
as one of the Abwehr's sub-agents. He was released and
made his number with van der Berg, winning his confidence
by giving him some messages which he wanted transmitted
to London. These were in fact fictitious ones planted by the
Germans with the object of tracing the transmitter. At first
Giskes had had his doubts about Ridderhof's claim to inside
information, but in the event the ruse worked. For with the
aid of direction-finders the transmitter was traced to a house
in Fahrenheit Street, The Hague.[29] Ridderhof unfortunately
was not the only Dutch traitor. Indeed one, van der Waals,
had already gone over to the Germans four months before
Ridderhof came on the scene, disclosing that there was a
secret wireless post in touch with Britain.[30]

The two Dutch SOE agents first parachuted into Holland
were Hubertus Lauwers and Thijs Taconis, and early in

March 1942 these two were arrested. It was inevitable that Lauwers who did the enciphering and transmitting should be required to transmit signals given to him by his captors.

It was about this time that instructions were given in London to those decoding signals received not to adhere too closely to the expected "handwriting" of an agent, when judging whether the signals were genuine, since variations could often be accounted for by transmitting in difficult clandestine conditions, in a hurry or when under exceptional strain. That relaxation would not by itself have brought about what later developed, but what proved absolutely disastrous was the failure to read the signals with an alert mind and pay attention to security checks.

Though closely watched, Lauwers sent the signal he was instructed to transmit, omitting his security check, but it is evident that this was overlooked or disregarded in Baker Street, the signal being accepted as genuine. (The security check took the form of an error in the sixteenth letter of the text.) The message sent ended with a request that supplies be dropped at Steenwijk Moor. To the astonishment of Lauwers, two days after receiving that signal, London transmitted a signal for the drop to take place.[31]

Lauwers, when next signalling, then decided to tell London in plain words that he had been caught. Though he had a guard standing over him and carrying a revolver, Lauwers managed to insert the word "caught" in his signal, not once but at least three times[32] and, according to a French report, four.[33] He did this with the use of nulls, so that an alert cipher clerk, extracting the nulls, would see that they spelt the word "caught" several times and would therefore be in no doubt about what had happened.[34] One would assume that the repeated word "caught" in addition to the absence of the security check could not possibly pass unnoticed. It seems almost incredible that these clear warnings could be ignored. Yet they were.

A joint Anglo-Dutch operation called "Operation Kern" was put into effect during the period from June 1942 to May 1943. The trap laid by Giskes was completely effective. Lauwers was instructed to transmit signals which he continued to do without his security check which Giskes did not even know. The result for the Allies was disaster. Messages which Baker Street assumed to be genuine came from Giskes. As a result of this game of "play-back", never more skilfully or more effectively developed, by the summer of 1942 there were thirty faked dropping zones[35] and sixteen fictitious sabotage groups[36] reported. The seventeen agents who were flown over and parachuted in accordance with the signals exchanged were all captured. Yet to Baker Street they seemed, from the results reported, to have been most successful in their operations and more agents were sent over. When bogus requests for such provisions as clothes, coffee and tobacco were received, five tons were sent.[37]

A large number of fictitious resistance fighters was reported, estimated to amount to about 1,500, and accordingly a quantity of explosives was sent over and dropped for their use in addition to 3,000 automatic pistols, 5,000 revolvers, 3,000 machine guns, 2,000 hand grenades and 500,000 rounds of ammunition, all of which fell into the hands of Giskes. Now that he had thoroughly deluded London, he had the game going wholly his own way, and when in February 1943 a team called "Operation Golf" arrived and were immediately arrested, a signal was sent to London, "All well".[38] It even reached the stage of the ludicrous when Richard Christmann, one of Giskes' men, was advised that he had been awarded the MC.[39] Even when a SOE agent, George Denning, managed to escape through France and Spain and reached London on 3rd September 1943 and told them of the arrests, London found it difficult to believe and thought that at least some of the radio links must still be genuine.[40]

Early in 1944 two agents, Peter Dourlein and Johan Ubbink, managed to escape and get to Madrid; they were taken to Gibraltar on 1st February 1944 and thence to London. There they were regarded as suspects and spent months in Brixton prison before they convinced those who questioned them.[41]

By the time the penny at last dropped in London, forty-seven of the fifty-two agents parachuted had been executed. In the whole resistance movement many thousands lost their lives, including 115,000 out of 140,000 Jews. "The

Netherlands", writes one outstanding authority on SOE, "bore an incomparably greater brunt of Nazi tyranny than any other enemy occupied territory in the West".[42]

At the end of March 1944, when it was all over, Giskes sent the following signal to London:

> To Messrs. Blunt Bingham* and Successors Ltd stop you are trying to make business in the Netherlands without our assistance stop we think this rather unfair in view of our long and successful co-operation as your sole agent stop but never mind whenever you will come to the continent you may be assured that you will be received with the same care and result as all those you sent us before stop so long.

One naturally wonders how London could have blundered so persistently and even whether an enemy agent could have got on to the staff of SOE. However, after the war a Dutch Parliamentary Commission of Inquiry was set up and completely rejected allegations of treachery. They referred to lack of experience and utter inefficiency and disregard of elementary security rules, and concluded that the disaster was brought by errors of judgement.[43]

No doubt there is always a temptation for those who have devised a system which seems to meet every requirement of planned security, to take something for granted, especially if it has been found to work satisfactorily elsewhere. Minds which should have noted the first absence of a security check and failed even to take in the repeated warning "caught", evidently suffered from casual over-confidence. They were far from alert. It was a sorry tale of utter carelessness that fell far short of the standard of vigilance usually maintained at SOE.

*   *   *   *

On occasion SOE agents were able to obtain and transmit information of value. Thus some of the intelligence available at Naval Intelligence in 1943 about the numbers and dispositions of U-boats was attributable to SOE operating in

* The names of the first and second directors of the Dutch section of SOE.

Bordeaux.[44] A more notable and valuable piece of intelligence forthcoming from Denmark contributed to the joint Anglo-American air attack on Peenemunde in the Baltic, no fewer than 150 bombers taking part, putting back Hitler's plan to flatten London with V-2s.[45]

SOE also contributed to making up the explosive charges that were used to destroy the dock gates at St Nazaire in March 1942, one of the most successful operations carried out by Combined Operations.[46]

But in the main the task of SOE was, and remained, to "set Europe ablaze" by various forms of sabotage and disruption of enemy movements and operations. Even such simple operations – simple, that is, subject to not being caught – as changing the labels on railway goods waggons could infuriate the enemy and cause confusion and delay, those intended for Lorient turning up at Strasbourg and those required at Calais arriving at Carcassone.

In the main, however, it was with acts of destruction that SOE were chiefly associated. Damage and on occasion destruction of power stations and transformers were prominent among the various activities; so was the demolition of locks on waterways, the destruction of bridges, and the disruption of arrangements for water supply. Transport was frequently attacked; ships were sunk in harbours and attacks were made on railways, not only the permanent way but trains carrying troops, especially in France, and those carrying oil wanted at U-boat bases.[47]

Factories with high priority in the enemy's industrial war effort were obvious targets. Thus, in Norway not only were the pyrite mines and plant at Orkla attacked but, even more important, the Skefko ball-bearing works at Oslo were virtually demolished. A single ball-bearing works can supply needs on the widest scale. Thus there was a period during the war when the destruction of one ball-bearing works in this country could have virtually grounded the whole of the RAF.[48] So the demolition of the Skefko works was a major and most effective achievement. A subsidiary action in the same field of war effort was the bringing out from Gothenburg of aircraft loaded with ball-bearings. Likewise a notable success was scored when the Ratier air screw factory at

Toulouse was blown up. Five ships, carrying no less than 25,000 tons of special steels, successfully ran the German blockade of Sweden under cover of a *haar* (sea mist), assisted by interference with telephone communications.[49]

Of all the single operations carried out by SOE almost certainly the most important and decisive was that against Germany's heavy water supply at Vemork in Norway. It was known as early as May 1940 that orders had been given to increase the production of heavy water (deuterium oxide) to 3,000 pounds a year, a basic requirement for the atomic bomb. After the failure of a glider-borne expedition in November 1941,* a Norwegian section of SOE was trained near Aviemore and subsequently attended a special training school near Cambridge. The leader of the attempt was Knut Haukelid who was so successful that he was able to send the following enciphered signal to London:[50]

High concentration installation at Vemork completely destroyed on the night of 27th/28th February stop Gunnerside [a colleague] has gone to Sweden stop greetings.

Though wireless communications were working well, Haukelid was well aware of the attempts by the enemy with direction-finders to ascertain his position, the mountainous nature of the country affording him some welcome protection. For safety's sake he discontinued regular communications with London.

Haukelid next received the following signal:

Most important to obtain most exact information about conditions and volume of present production at Vemork and Notodden stop when is final production expected to commence stop how is the plant transported stop imi† when was the production process resumed end.

As a result of Haukelid's reply American bombers launched an attack on 16th November 1943. It was successful

---

* This was the one on which the sixteen British men surrendered and were afterwards executed (mentioned on page 160).

† "Imi" in telegraphy indicates a mark of interrogation.

and convinced the Germans that continuation of production there was not practicable, and on 29th January 1944, London sent another signal, reporting that they understood that the heavy water apparatus at Vemork and Rjukan was to be dismantled and transported to Germany. Haukelid was asked if he could confirm if this was true and, if so, how would he suggest preventing transport.

Haukelid replied that Vemork was well guarded and that the best chance was to sink the ferry. He and Einar, one of his colleagues, recognized that such an operation must inevitably cost Norwegian lives and London was asked if this was necessary. The reply left them in no doubt that it certainly was. In such circumstances there is always a temptation to drop word to some acquaintance who must become a casualty if he is to go on board; such an action always runs the risk of acting as a tip-off to the enemy, however, and Haukelid and his companion resisted the temptation. They managed to place the charge well forward in the ship so that the rudder and propeller would rise. The charge of nineteen pounds of high explosive was timed to go off at 10.45 a.m. when the ferry would be over the deepest water. Everything went according to plan. The heavy water, carried on board in some seventy large drums, went down with the ferry. So unfortunately did twenty-six passengers but twenty-seven others were saved.[51] Four of the drums were later salvaged.[52] The date was 20th February 1944.

No single operation carried out by SOE was so vital to Britain. But for this the first atomic bomb might well have fallen on London and not on Hiroshima.

*   *   *   *

Less than twelve months after Hitler's promise to respect the neutrality of Denmark he sent in his troops. Nobody treated the enemy with more hauteur than King Christian, a big man not only in stature who, to Hitler's suggestion that the two countries be ruled as one, replied that really he was a bit old to rule Germany as well; and when later von Ribbentrop asked him to include two Danish Nazis in his cabinet, the King's snappy reply was, "There are no Danish Nazis".

Resistance began to develop but until the spring of 1942 Mogens Hammer was the sole SOE agent in Denmark and he had difficulty setting up a wireless post. A link was therefore arranged with London through one Ebbe Munck, in Sweden.[53] SOE's role in Denmark was, however, a very limited one. Most of the resistance activities took the form of destruction or obstruction – digging up cobbled roadways, overturning trams, lighting bonfires in the streets, strikes in factories and on the railways and in the power stations, plunging the place into darkness at night, and generally wrecking the industrial effort which might otherwise have been put by the enemy to his own use.

In Yugoslavia SOE agents were active when Prince Paul and his pro-Axis government were chased out of office on 26th March 1941 and General Simovic assumed responsibility for government on behalf of the young King Peter.[54] Hitler's fury was quickly demonstrated in the fierce bombing of Belgrade by the German Air Force, and German troops entered the country at various points. In Serbia, the little-known Colonel Draza Mihailovic assumed control of guerilla formations which were in action from April of that year.* Thousands of tons of supplies were sent to the Partisans by SOE, mostly by sea.[57] The Yugoslavs suffered frightful cruelty at the hands of the Germans. But there were occasions when they repaid the enemy in his own coin, and who can blame them? SOE agents blocked the Danube from mid-April to mid-June 1941 by sinking ships laden with concrete and other heavy material.[58]

Czechoslovakian intelligence was principally in the hands of General Moravec, the head of the exiled Czechoslovakian

* SOE withdrew Brigadier Armstrong's mission to Mihailovic in May 1944 and OSS withdrew theirs in October of the same year. It may be, as has been suggested,[55] that after Stalingrad Mihailovic saw the writing on the wall and sought to conserve the strength of the Royalist Cetniks against the threat of Communism. It was at the Teheran Conference in November 1943 that Churchill and Roosevelt agreed to Stalin's demand to support Tito. British Officers who later had the task of arresting Mihailovic and his henchmen and handing them over to Tito found it a most distasteful duty. In May 1945 9,000 Cetniks and 3,000 women and children fought their way through the Partisans in Slovenia into Allied lines where they asked that their arms be used against the Russians.[56] They were disarmed and interned in Italy.

force of 3,000 men in Britain. The signals section was first sited at Dulwich but was soon bombed out and was moved to Woldingham. It was with a form of invisible ink invented by Professor Locarde of Lyons that signals were exchanged with agents who carried out the murder of Heydrich.[59] The Czechoslovaks enjoyed the distinction of being allowed to operate their own cipher and code service in Britain. The same applied to the Poles[60] who unfortunately were too distant from us to enable much help to be sent.

It was principally in France that the activities of SOE were developed on a major scale. Colonel Buckmaster of the French section has this comment to make:[61]

> SOE did undoubtedly outwit the German Intelligence. For instance, more than 300 parachute operations, bringing arms and equipment to French patriots, took place in the south-west region of France during the period of January 1943 to June 1944 *without enemy interference.*

Activities reached their peak on the night of 5th June 1944 when Allied forces crossed the Channel and opened the Second Front in Normandy. As always happens immediately before a major military operation, there was a sudden increase in the number of signals – more than five hundred on the night of 5th June to more than fifty SOE operators.[62] There was a stream of personal messages, all carrying pre-arranged meanings and calling for action. Hearts were lifted as at last it was sensed that the great day had arrived.

Two signals in particular have secured their place in history, both taken from a poem by Verlaine. The first was: *"Les sanglots longs des violons d'automne"* (the long sobs of the violins of autumn) which told the agents whose tasks were to disrupt railway communications to stand by.

The second was: *"Bercent mon coeur d'une langueur monotone"* (rocking my heart with a monotonous weariness) which told those agents to act.

It is believed that the enemy had in some way got hold of the true meanings of those signals; if so, an informer may have been at work. We are told that the signals had originally been allocated to another agent's circuit and that one or both of them may have fallen into enemy hands. Though the German Fifth Army had been alerted, fortunately there had been so many false alarms that adequate heed was not paid. In any case the signals did not reveal the assault area.

Equipped in advance by SOE, the various resistance armies in France by this time numbered as many as about 120,000 men.[63]

In the first week of operations 960 railway demolitions were put into effect out of a planned total of 1,055. In addition many road and telegraphic communications were disrupted. Every single train leaving Marseilles and Lyons for the North was derailed, some of them more than once.[64] One of the enemy's units ordered to go immediately to Normandy was a Panzer division stationed in the neighbourhood of the Pyrenées; with roads disrupted and bridges destroyed, the arrival of the division was considerably delayed;[65] meantime the invading Allies were securing and enlarging their bridgehead.

The dislocation of railway communications continued; indeed by the end of July a total of 668 locomotives had been destroyed and the number of attacks on the permanent way had reached no fewer than 2,900.[66]

In the South of France some units of the *Armée Secrète* went into action before the date planned for them to do so. It had been intended that they await the Allied landing in the South of France, and this did not take place till 15th August, only ten days before the liberation of Paris. The eagerness of the units to go into action cost them heavily in casualties,[67] but it undoubtedly helped to delay the enemy's efforts to bring reinforcements from the South to Normandy and so assisted the Allied armies to push further inland.

*   *   *   *

At no time in history have secret armies and resistance movements played such a large part in war. Some like the Poles were geographically ill-placed and suffered frightful casualties; the story of their valour and their tragedy is too little appreciated. But of those movements which could be provided with direct and continuous aids, SOE stands out as one of the major contributions to the intense and widespread irregular warfare which our Chiefs of Staff learnt to respect and appreciate, just as the American Chiefs of Staff came to value the work of OSS.

In this review of SOE we have concerned ourselves principally with the communications system and linked administrative arrangements with mention of activities in the field sufficient to indicate the performance and value of the service provided by Baker Street. To put things in perspective, however, it is right to record that the greater part of the work in the field, with all its dangers, was carried out by nationals of those countries or "half nationals" who spoke the language without any trace of English accent. If we were telling the whole story of SOE, we should be entitled to claim for Britain's share only that it helped. The Baker Street headquarters provided the administration, the training establishments, the arms and equipment, the planning of operations and the signal service.

The performance of the cryptosystems and the signal service was unquestionably effective. One has only to consider what happened in the Netherlands where it failed, to appreciate how well it worked elsewhere, never better than in France during the twelve months prior to D-Day and in the immediate aftermath. But for SOE the task of the Allies, when they opened the Second Front, would have been harder, perhaps even much harder; and but for SOE London might have been the target for the first atomic bomb.

TEN

FINALE

A comprehensive and detailed history of ciphers and codes used in the Second World War would take note of certain feats of individuals and countries that have not concerned us, like the Hungarian, Major Bibo, who is credited with having cracked ciphers much as other people crack walnuts, and the Swedes who occupied a ring-side seat and read the signals of participants, including those of Russia, Germany, Britain and America.

In this study, however, we have confined ourselves to successes and failures in the hidden war of ciphers and codes, seen against the background of military and naval operations. It remains to draw the threads together and see what conclusions can reasonably be formed about the contributions to the Allied victory made by secret communications and their unravelment.

It cannot be said that in their standards of security the nations of the Western world distinguished themselves, either in the years immediately leading up to the war or even during certain phases of it. In diplomatic offices telephone conversations were carried on about secret matters, even in countries that were police states where it was obvious that telephones were tapped, and confidential waste paper was allowed to fall into the hands of agents; no thought was given to the lives of enemies of the Nazi régime, like von Hassel, or of the Fascists, like Barzini. Keys of embassies were obtained and wax impressions made on the justified assumption that the staff would not trouble about changing locks; and sometimes, even when it was known that access to a safe had been gained, nothing was done about it.

Even if reasonable standards of security had been maintained on diplomatic premises, however, tin-openers to ciphers would still have been found, though not so easily. Moreover, it is well established and indeed known to every student of cryptography that the more a cipher is used, the less its security. If systems are used for too long, the lights are always red. Yet in a single day, SHAEF (Supreme Headquarters Allied Expeditionary Force) enciphered material totalling over 9,000,000 words. Without knowing the circumstances at the time we cannot say how much reduction could have been made, but several million words a day had before then become quite common, and it is obvious that the use of cipher systems was reckless and completely disregarded security.

Sometimes ciphers were used where ordinary plain text would have done or even no message at all. On one occasion Anthony Eden (later Earl of Avon), then Foreign Secretary, returned from a visit to Washington; shortly afterwards he received a message from the British Ambassador there, thanking him for his services and expressing delight at his safe return. Since he had no doubt expressed his thanks before the Foreign Secretary left and could hardly have been disappointed at his safe return, one might think that the use of cipher for such a purpose could have been dispensed with and security given precedence over courtesy. But the height of frivolity belongs to the Germans whose cipher on one occasion was used for nothing more serious than to convey birthday greetings.[1]

It is common – indeed much too common – to make unjustified assumptions about security. One system after another was thought to be proof against unravelment; this applied to both sides in the war and to both military and naval systems. The conclusion must surely be that the only system which could rightly be regarded as unbreakable is the one-time random pad, because it undermines the only basic means of breaking ciphers. The Germans thought the Enigma system safe, so much so that at one time they were using it to send over 2,000 signals a day;[2] yet a young cryptanalyst, assisted by a team, unravelled it, just as the Americans discovered the key to the Japanese cipher, Purple. Kahn lists the ciphers of thirty-three countries and the Vatican which, he says, were read by the Germans;[3] many were neutral countries and those with small budgets to spend on cipher services no doubt had difficulty competing. The Germans were certainly skilful. There is no equivalent estimate of British successes though, referring to the period November-December 1941, Kahn deduced that solutions totalled about 300 a week.[4] (These included Japanese ones, but not Purple.)

Difficulties arose from exceptional achievements in breaking ciphers which the enemy considered safe, principally that of Britain in unravelling and keeping abreast of Enigma, and that of America in regard to Purple. As it turned out, the distribution of the Ultra secrets and the arrangements made to secure their safety seem to have worked out as nearly perfectly as one could wish.

Of all the communications secrets in the war, that of Ultra proved much the most beneficial. For a fuller appreciation, the reader is referred to Winterbotham's book. We can, however, get a fair appraisal of what it meant, if we cast our minds back to the First World War where there was no equivalent achievement. A general then had to judge what the enemy would do next as best he could. As Field Marshal Wilson once said: "One had to put one's cap on back to front, sit the other side of the table, pretend to be the enemy as things looked to him, and judge his next move." With Ultra at the disposal of Allied generals, there was no need for any such exercises of imagination, for the information was available. Thus, when von Kluge took over from von Rundstedt on the Western Front, he sent a signal to the High Command in Berlin, giving everything the Allies needed to know, a complete inventory of units and their strength.[5] There was a period in the latter part of the war when our knowledge of the German Air Force on the Western Front extended to the ages of the crews and their experience (by then usually slight) and, if memory serves, even the identity of one or two of their path-finders.[6] It became almost a one-way old pals club.*

* While it is beyond question that, from 1941 on, we read many hundreds of the enemy's signals and acquired a great deal of detail, it must be borne in mind that, pending release of official information, it is im-

As Field Marshal Alexander remarked, advance knowledge of the enemy's strength, disposition and intentions brought a new dimension to prosecuting war. Churchill expressed the view that Ultra was decisive.[7] Its use on a world-wide scale must have been unique.

Quite a different type of achievement was that of MI5 in turning German agents, feeding them with the information which it suited the Allies that the enemy should have. There was nothing new in double agents; their first appearance in history must have been long ago. But the feat of rounding up the substantial army of enemy agents – virtually 100 per cent successful – and using a good half of them to hoodwink the enemy constituted a new means, at least on such a scale, of making use of the enemy's own cipher communications system. The intricacies of planning the wealth of bogus signals to lend credence to the "shadow" invasion force in the Dover area was a masterpiece. Farago's investigations of the Abwehr records leaves no doubt that on that score Britain won all along the line.

What surely stands out above all other lessons for Britain to remember now and always is to be learnt from the Battle of the Atlantic. During the period when Admiralty signals were being read by the enemy but those of the enemy remained unbroken, things went hard for Britain. Indeed the first ten days of March 1943 brought us closer to defeat than at any other period of the war. Nobody can read the story of the Battle of the Atlantic without concluding that the result hung principally on the battle of ciphers. Various inventions played their part and other services gave their help. But could radar or direction-finders have saved Britain, if the struggle between the cipher teams had gone the other way? If the Admiralty's signals had remained open to the enemy, and if his had remained a closed book, nothing could have

---

possible to say which information came from reading one or other of the Enigma Keys. Many signals in other ciphers were also read. Some intercepts were read only partly, difficulties arising from changing frequencies, interference and other causes. In addition it is also possible that we listened-in to scrambled telephone conversations; and of course some information came from agents and even from prisoners of war. Beesly tells how successful Rodger Winn (later Lord Justice Winn) was in forecasting the enemy's moves.

saved the day.

One can argue likewise about the Battle of Britain. When our troops were brought back from Dunkirk, they were without arms, and we were faced with the prospect of a German invasion of our island. The view of the official historian of the war at sea is that the enemy lacked the resources to gain sufficient command of the sea and that, had the expedition set sail, a British naval victory would have been the certain result.[8] An opposite view, however, is that naval forces could not operate successfully in confined waters against land-based aircraft and that, if the RAF had been eliminated, our warships could not have survived the weight of attack by German aircraft.[9] Certainly Cunningham's respect for dive-bombing[10] and the fate of ships like the *Prince of Wales* and the *Repulse* under attack from Japanese dive-bombers, and likewise of the Japanese warships at the hands of American carrier-borne aircraft at the Battle of Midway, cannot be disregarded. To some of our senior Staff Officers it seemed that RAF Fighter Command alone stood between us and defeat. Dowding's skill in husbanding that small force while turning back enemy bombers was a feat of decisive importance; he had the advantage of being kept posted with enemy signals which provided him with their intelligence.

Hitler always admitted that in espionage Germany could not match Russia. The obtainment of highly secret information on such a scale, and its transmission in cipher which defied the wits of cryptanalysts, was a major contributor to the ultimate success of the Red Army. (In the ciphers used within their espionage service the standard of security was excellent; it was in the administrative direction that security failed.) In a strictly military sense it may be questioned whether the Russians could have defeated the Germans, even though Stalin was a far bigger man than Hitler and made only one major mistake, that of refusing to heed the warnings of the attack in June 1941.* (Hitler made frequent mistakes, ordering attacks by units that were non-operational or even

---

* We do not know how many warnings were known to Stalin himself; some may have been withheld from him by those who hesitated to tell him what he had already declined to accept.

non-existent, ordering his generals to perform the impossible, and disrupting operations by the U-boats.) If the Russians had not been kept so well posted with the enemy's plans, they might still have exhausted them in the end; but in such circumstances it might well have taken them considerably longer to accomplish that feat, especially if they had lost their oil fields, and their roll of fatal casualties, already horrifyingly high, would have been higher still.*

The development of direction-finders killed the system of using espionage agents in enemy occupied territory to transmit regularly from fixed addresses. By contrast, the use of agents to obtain the keys to ciphers and codes was the outstanding achievement of the Italian, Amé. Ciano's catalogue of systems read is certainly impressive with the American Black Code, used in Cairo, one of the more notable. But for the advice of Barzini, how many more secret communications between Churchill and Roosevelt would have been known to the enemy? On the German side, the activities of their agent, Hans Thomsen, were certainly fruitful; and they were provided by Cicero with much secret material. The trade in ciphers that developed and some of the high prices offered for them underline the important part they played. Britain's SIS produced some gratifying results: the keys to an Italian submarine code, to a code used by Italian surface vessels and to the Vichy diplomatic system, to the Abwehr's hand system of enciphering and, most of all, to a German naval cipher, possibly Enigma, at a crucial stage of the war. Valuable contributions were made by Donovan and his OSS, notably at the time of Torch, but also revealing the deals done in ciphers at the Finnish Embassy in Stockholm.

Of SOE, it is not easy to be specific about adding up their contribution. Even without outside assistance, such was the

---

* Total fatal casualties, civilian included, are estimated at about 50,000,000, the Russian totalling 20,000,000. The Poles may have lost 6,000,000, the Germans 4,500,000 and the Yugoslavs 1,750,000. The Jews probably lost 5,500,000 lives. British fatal casualties were about 450,000, French about the same, Italian 410,000, Americans 290,000, Greeks over 250,000, and Dutch over 200,000, mostly civilian. The Empire overseas lost 120,000 lives. Figures are approximate and disputable.[11]

spirit of patriots in occupied countries that they would have undoubtedly made life as uncomfortable and difficult as they could for occupying forces. But the signal service did beyond doubt contribute materially to the ultimate success, and it says much for those who were responsible for devising their systems that signals could be boldly broadcast and yet retain their security. Some of those who like digging for dirt seem to have made a set at SOE, but the organization, guidance and planned operations, and the constant intelligence service embodied therein constituted an achievement which must surely be acclaimed.

We cannot but conclude that cipher and code services played a vital part. They helped our small Fighter Command to win the Battle of Britain and ultimately they saved us from defeat in the Battle of the Atlantic. They enabled the Allies to outgeneral the Germans on land and to outwit the Japanese at sea. They were of inestimable value to the Russians, and they enabled resistance movements and secret armies to carry out organized operations of great value to the regular services. In addition they became an important pursuit of espionage agents. In sum, they played a far bigger part in influencing the fortunes of war than in any previous major conflict.

In sizing up the performances of the various countries, it is tempting to look for some sort of batting order, but in making comparisons we should not always be comparing like with like. While the British success in reading Enigma stands out as unique in military history, the performance of B-Dienst was extraordinarily and consistently successful during the first half of the war. The Americans, with their series of "Magics", in particular that of unravelling Purple, were brilliant. Perhaps the most gratifying reflection of all is the fact that Britain and America were allies in a way in which Germany and Italy never were; the sharing of their cipher secrets demonstrated the true trust and friendship that bound them together and contributed to their ultimate success.

Of the Russians we can say that in the construction of ciphers that suited their espionage network they showed the highest skill and, incidentally, reminded us that there was still room for the old pencil-and-paper systems and that machines were not suitable to all circumstances. In a tightly controlled police state the inadequate security in administration of the signals service may seem surprising but it was no doubt due, at least in part, to the 1938 purge. The general standard of their field communications, which in the fighting against Finland in 1939-40 was poor, was considerably improved later. We know little of the standard of their cipher-breaking (as distinct from acquiring keys by other means) but, as we have seen, they do not seem to have broken Enigma unless it was in the last phase of the war.*

The Italians have long been among the leading nations in the field of cryptography, dating back at least to the Renaissance; their systems traditionally have a certain character of their own with a substitution cipher as the basis, super-enciphered in a transposition system. With Amé's team of accomplished agents and keys to embassies, they were well provided and must have imposed on their cryptanalysis less of a burden than they would otherwise have done. Not enough is known of the cipher service of the Free French to enable us to form a view. Traditionally, France is one of the most advanced and skilful leaders, and we can only suppose that, if circumstances had been different, she would have held her own.

To sum up: in the earlier stages both British and American codes were read by the Germans, and in their fighting in 1939-40 the Russian field ciphers were also read. But as the war progressed, the enemy lost their advantage. It is a fair conclusion that no country came out of the cipher war better than Britain and it is questionable whether any did as well.

In drawing such conclusions as these, we must bear in mind that at the outbreak of war there was no supreme cipher authority in this country. Each of the armed forces had their own authority, the Foreign Office theirs, and so on; it was not till 1944 that the need for a central authority became accepted. The same applied to the Americans who reached the same conclusion. In Germany it was even more

* On 30th July 1944 a U-boat was sunk in the Gulf of Finland; it was later raised by the Russians who recovered an Enigma machine.[12]

fragmented, a position considerably worsened by the intense, and often bitter, rivalries that existed. It is an interesting reflection whether, had each of these countries operated a central controlling authority from the start, it would have made a material difference to the security of their cryptosystems. As things were, probably at least half, and perhaps over half, the systems used by these countries were read by others from whom they were intended to be kept secret. For what it is worth, my own view is that a really tight standard of security is impossible without integration.

It does not of course follow that judgements of what ended more than thirty years ago still apply. Moreover, there have been technical developments, and a number of what were novelties in the war soon became obsolete after it. Within ten years of the end of hostilities high-speed transmission had come into being, so that a signal would produce no more than a swift blur; not that that was enough to secure the safety of agents, as the Portland spy ring discovered. Microphotography became developed so that a closely-typed foolscap sheet could be reduced to less than the size of a pin's head. The use of satellites has become commonplace, but information that cannot be photographed still requires a form of transmission, and the use of ciphers and codes seems certain to continue. The same no doubt applies to invisible ink and telephone scramblers. Further than these few observations, however, we cannot go, for the future remains, as always, the great unknown.

We began our story by looking back at the pre-war years, the Thirties when Britain slept, when embassies knowingly employed foreign spies on their staffs, when keys to ciphers remained unchanged, and when our codes used too long by the Royal Navy became mere reading matter to others. We noted the cost of our unpreparedness and how perilously close to defeat we came. At the time many people did not realize it and, when France fell, they contented themselves with the comforting reflection that: "There are no more allies to let us down now." They did not know that we were almost, but not quite, naked of arms with 660 operational fighter aircraft and a handful of tanks. It was estimated that there were only about 70,000 rifles in the country. Faith bore us up and leadership was inspired. But those who knew something of the peril in which we then stood would shudder to see this country again in such an extremity.

We should conclude by considering whether we have remembered the bitter lessons which we had to learn in the early days of the war. Today we have Russia, whose Navy scarcely took part in the war, equipped with a submarine force which is certainly not needed for defence but is about as great as anything Doenitz had at his command; and each month it grows larger. When Mrs Thatcher drew attention to this, the Minister of Defence then in office brushed it aside. We live and learn, so we are told, and no doubt many of us perform both functions; but evidently not all. Only six years after the end of the war the strength of Naval Intelligence had been reduced by disposing of forty-nine out of every fifty posts of the war-time strength.[13] No doubt a considerable reduction was to be expected, but with these figures in mind, we may well wonder what the strength of it is now and can only hope that it is sufficient. For we are an island race and command of our sea lanes is essential to our survival.

For those who are concerned with cost, it may be said that a first-class intelligence service is a rare bargain. As an example, we are told that the cost to the Russians of maintaining their network in Switzerland during the war was no more than that of producing one medium-heavy tank.[14] In our Government budgets no separate provision is made for cipher services, but for 1976-7 the inclusive estimate for "foreign and other secret services" was twenty-eight million pounds or about fifty pence per head of the population, less than the price of a packet of cigarettes.

The cost of maintaining intelligence and security services equipped with the best of cryptographic specialists is therefore negligible. The cost of failing to do so could be disastrous.

Timetable of the Main Events of the War

1939

1 Sept.	Germany attacks Poland. Ultimatum from Britain and France
3 Sept.	Britain and France declare war on Germany
17 Sept.	Russia occupies East Poland
27 Sept.	Surrender of Warsaw
28 Sept.	Poland partitioned between Germany and Russia
30 Nov.	Russia invades Finland

1940

13 March	Peace signed between Finland and Russia
9 April	Germany invades Denmark and Norway
10 April	British expedition leaves for Norway
8 May	British forces sent to occupy Iceland
10 May	Germany invades Netherlands, Belgium and Luxembourg
	Neville Chamberlain resigns, Winston Churchill succeeds him
12 May	Germany invades France
14 May	Cease-fire in Netherlands
17 May	Fall of Brussels
19 May	Gamelin dismissed, Weygand succeeds him
25 May	Fall of Boulogne
27 May	Fall of Calais. Evacuation of British forces from Dunkirk begins

28 May	Belgium surrenders
3 June	Evacuation of British forces from Dunkirk completed
10 June	Italy declares war on Britain and France
14 June	Fall of Paris
15, 16 June	Russia occupies Baltic States
22 June	France surrenders
27 June	Romania cedes Bessarabia and Northern Bukovina to Russia
3 July	British attack French fleet at Oran and Mers-el-Kebir
10 July	Battle of Britain begins
19 July	SOE established
2 Sept.	America exchanges fifty destroyers for bases in West Indies
7 Sept.	Night air attacks on London begin
15 Sept.	Biggest daylight air attack on Britain; GAF lose fifty-six aircraft
27 Sept.	German-Italian-Japanese Tripartite Pact signed
28 Oct.	Italy invades Greece
8 Nov.	British offensive in Libya begins
11 Nov.	British attack Italian fleet at Taranto
14 Nov.	Coventry attacked by GAF
20-25 Nov.	Hungary, Romania and Czechoslovakia join Tripartite Pact
9 Dec.	First British offensive in North Africa begins
29 Dec.	City of London attacked by GAF

1941

22 Jan.	British take Tobruk
1 March	Bulgaria joins Tripartite Pact
10-11 March	First SOE agent parachuted into France
11 March	Lease-Lend Act signed by Roosevelt
13-14 March	Clyde attacked by GAF
26 March	General Simovic takes over in Yugoslavia
28 March	Battle of Cape Matapan
30 March	Germans launch counter-offensive in North Africa

5 April	British forces diverted from North Africa to Greece
6 April	German invasion of Yugoslavia and Greece
11 April	Russo-Japanese Treaty of Neutrality signed
10 May	Last major night attack on London by GAF. Hess flies to Scotland
24 May	*Hood* sunk
27 May	*Bismarck* sunk
1 June	British withdraw from Crete
8 June	Allies enter Syria
14 June	Roosevelt freezes Axis funds in America
18 June	German-Turkish Treaty of Friendship signed
22 June	Germany invades Russia
14 Aug.	Atlantic Charter signed
17 Aug.	Germans take 650,000 prisoners at Kiev
25 Aug.	British and Russian forces enter Iran
8 Sept.	Leningrad isolated
18 Sept.	Fall of Kiev
18 Nov.	British launch offensive in Libya
7 Dec.	Japanese attack American Pacific fleet at Pearl Harbour
8 Dec.	Japanese attack Thailand and Malaya
10 Dec.	*Prince of Wales* and *Repulse* sunk. China declares war on Germany and Japan
11 Dec.	Germany and Italy declare war on America
17 Dec.	Japanese invade Sarawak
22 Dec.	Japanese invade Philippines
23 Dec.	Japanese take Wake
26 Dec.	Fall of Hong Kong. First Washington conference

1942

2 Jan.	Japanese capture Manila
3 Jan.	Japanese invade Borneo
Jan.	U-boats attack ships in American ports
10 Jan.	Fall of Kuala Lumpur
21 Jan.	German counter-offensive in North Africa. Japanese land on New Guinea and Solomon Islands

15 Feb.	Surrender of Singapore
19 Feb.	Japanese bomb Darwin
27-29 Feb.	Battle of Java Sea
2 March	Japanese take Batavia
9 March	Fall of Rangoon
18 March	Commando raid on St Nazaire
6-8 May	Battle of Coral Sea
27 May	Defeat of Russians at Kharkov
30 May	RAF bombers attack Cologne in force
June	Siege of Malta reaches crisis
4 June	Battle of Midway Island
21 June	Germans take Tobruk
25 June	Eisenhower appointed C-in-C in Europe
28 June	Germans take Sebastopol
1 July	Rommel held at El Alamein
23 July	Germans take Rostov
25-27 July	Second Washington Conference
7 Aug.	Americans land on Guadalcanal
12 Aug.	First Moscow Conference
19 Aug.	Commando raid on Dieppe
6 Sept.	Germans held at Stalingrad
23 Oct.-	Battle of El Alamein, decisive defeat of Axis
4 Nov.	forces
7 Nov.	Operation Torch: Allies land in North-West Africa
11 Nov.	Germans occupy Southern France
19-21 Nov.	Russian counter-offensive, Stalingrad encircled
11 Nov.	Germans enter unoccupied France
28 Nov.	Von Manstein orders withdrawal from Stalingrad

1943

3 Jan.	Germans' retreat from Caucasus begins
4 Jan.	Japanese begin evacuation of Guadalcanal
14-24 Jan.	Casablanca Conference
31 Jan.	Von Paulus surrenders at Stalingrad
March	Battle of Atlantic reaches crisis
11-17 May	Third Washington Conference
12 May	Organized German resistance in Tunisia ends

5 July	Battle of Kursk begins
9-10 July	Allied invasion of Sicily
25 July	Mussolini dismissed, Badoglio succeeds him
17-24 Aug.	First Quebec Conference
17 Aug.	Allies capture Messina
23 Aug.	Russians recover Kharkov
3 Sept.	Invasion of Italian mainland begins
8 Sept.	Italy surrenders
9 Sept.	Allies land at Salerno
10 Sept.	Germans occupy Rome
12 Sept.	Mussolini rescued by Germans
25 Sept.	Russians recapture Smolensk
1 Oct.	Allies capture Naples
13 Oct.	Italy declares war on Germany
18 Oct.-1 Nov.	Second Moscow Conference
1 Nov.	Americans land on Bougainville
6 Nov.	Russians recapture Kiev
22-26 Nov.	First Cairo Conference
28 Nov.-1 Dec.	Teheran Conference
4-6 Dec.	Second Cairo Conference
26 Dec.	*Scharnhorst* sunk

1944

18 Jan.	Battle of Cassino begins
22-23 Jan.	Allies land at Anzio
20 Feb.	Sinking of Germany's heavy water supply from Vemork
17 March	Cassino falls to Allies
18 March	RAF drop 3,000 tons of HE on Hamburg
19 March	German troops cross Hungarian frontier
2 April	Russians enter Romania
10 April	Russians recapture Odessa
22 April	Americans land on Dutch New Guinea
9 May	Russians recapture Sebastopol
17 May	Allies capture Cassino
4 June	Allies enter Rome

6 June	D-Day: Allied invasion of Normandy
13 June	First V-1s fired at London
18 June	American bombers attack Tokyo
27 June	Allies capture Cherbourg
3 July	Russians recapture Minsk
9 July	Allies capture Caen. Americans capture Saipan
20 July	Unsuccessful bomb plot to kill Hitler
1 Aug.	Warsaw rising
8 Aug.	Americans take Guam
15 Aug.	Allies invade Southern France
25 Aug.	Paris liberated
31 Aug.	Russians take Bucharest
3 Sept.	Brussels liberated
4 Sept.	Allies take Antwerp. End of Finnish-Russian fighting
5 Sept.	Russians declare war on Bulgaria
8 Sept.	V2s fired at London
10 Sept.	Second Quebec Conference
17 Sept.	Allied air-borne forces attack Arnheim
19 Sept.	Finland signs armistice
2 Oct.	Warsaw patriots surrender
14 Oct.	Athens liberated
20 Oct.	Russians and Tito's partisans enter Belgrade Americans land on Philippines
21-22 Oct.	Battle of Leyte Gulf
23-26 Oct.	Russians enter East Prussia
12 Nov.	*Tirpitz* sunk
16 Dec.	German counter-offensive on Ardennes (Battle of the Bulge) begins

1945

8 Jan.	Hitler authorizes limited withdrawals on Western Front
17 Jan.	Russians take Warsaw
22 Jan.	Burmah Road reopened
28 Jan.	End of Battle of the Bulge
3 Feb.	Americans land on Manila
4-12 Feb.	Yalta Conference

4 March	Finland declares war on Germany as from 15 Sept. 1944
6 March	Allies take Cologne
16 March	Americans take Iwo Jima
1 April	Allies enter Ruhr. Americans land on Okinawa
12 April	Death of Roosevelt: Truman becomes President
13 April	Russians enter Vienna. Allies capture Belsen and Buchenwald
28 April	Mussolini executed by partisans
29 April	Allies take Dachau and Milan
30 April	Hitler commits suicide
1 May	Doenitz takes command of German armed forces
2 May	Russians enter Berlin. German armies in Italy surrender
3 May	Allies enter Rangoon
8 May	VE Day. Germany acknowledges defeat
13 May	Russians enter Czechoslovakia
26 May	Royal Navy joins US Navy in Pacific
21 June	Americans take Okinawa
17 July	Potsdam Conference
27 July	Attlee becomes Prime Minister
6 Aug.	Atomic bomb dropped on Hiroshima
8 Aug.	Russia declares war on Japan
9 Aug.	Atomic bomb dropped on Nagasaki
14 Aug.	Japan surrenders

Sources of Information

A number of the books mentioned below have been published in more than one edition; the editions given are those to which page references refer. Although some writers who were in the Services have not given their ranks, I have included them where known.

Accoce, Pierre and Quet, Pierre, *The Lucy Spy Ring,* W. H. Allen, 1967.

Arnold-Forster, M. *The World at War,* Fontana-Collins, 1976.

Avon, Earl of, *The Eden Diaries,* Cassell, 1965.

Beesly, Patrick, *Very Special Intelligence: The Story of the Admiralty's Operational Intelligence Centre 1939-45,* Hamish Hamilton, 1977.

Brissaud, André, *Canaris,* Weidenfeld and Nicholson, 1974.

Broome, Captain Jack, *Convoy to Scatter,* William Kimber, 1972.

Bryans, J. L., *Blind Victory,* Skeffington, 1951.

Buckmaster, Colonel M. J., *They Fought Alone,* Odhams, 1958.

Busch, Harald, *U-boats at War,* Putnam, 1955.

Butler, Ewan, *Amateur Agent,* Harrap, 1963.

Butler, Sir J. R. M., *The Grand Strategy,* H.M.S.O.

Cadogan, Sir A., *The Cadogan Diaries,* ed. D. Dilks, Cassell, 1971.

Calvocoressi, P. & Wint, G., *Total War,* Allen Lane the Penguin Press, 1972.

Carell, Paul, (A) *Scorched Earth,* Harrap, 1970. (B) *Foxes of the Desert,* Macmillan, 1961.

Chandos, Lord, *Memoirs,* Bodley-Head, 1962.

Churchill, Peter, (A) *Of Their Own Choice,* Hodder & Stoughton, 1952. (B) *Duel of Wits,* Elmfield Press, 1974.

Churchill, W. S., *The Grand Alliance,* Cassell, 1950.

Ciano's Diary, 1939-43, Heinemann, 1947.

Ciano's Diplomatic Papers, ed. M. Muggeridge, Odhams Press, 1948.

Cockerill, A. W., *Sir Percy Sillitoe,* W. H. Allen, 1975.

Collier, Basil, *Defence of the United Kingdom,* H.M.S.O., 1957

Colvin, Ian, *Canaris, Chief of Intelligence,* George Mann, 1973.

Cookridge, E. H., (A) *Inside SOE,* Arthur Barker, 1966. (B) *The Third Man,* Arthur Barker, 1968. (C) *Gehlen, Spy of the Century,* Hodder and Stoughton, 1971. (D) *Secrets of the British Secret Service,* Sampson Low, Marston, 1948. (E) *Soviet Spy Net,* Frederick Muller, 1955.

Cox, Major Sir Geoffrey, *The Road to Trieste,* Heinemann, 1947.

Creighton, Rear-Admiral Kenelm, *Convoy Commodore,* William Kimber, 1956.

Cresswell, Captain John, *The Sea Warfare,* Regents of University of California, 1967.

Cunningham, Admiral of the Fleet Viscount, *Odyssey of a Sailor,* Hutchinson, 1951.

Dahlerus, Birger, *The Last Attempt,* Hutchinson, 1948.

Dallin, David J., *Soviet Espionage,* Oxford University Press, 1955.

Dalton, Hugh, *The Fateful Years,* Frederick Muller, 1957.

Deacon, Richard, (A) *A History of the British Secret Service,* Frederick Muller, 1969. (B) *A History of the Russian Secret Service;* Frederick Muller, 1972.

Deakin, F. W. & Storry, G. R., *The Case of Richard Sorge,* Chatto & Windus, 1966.

Dickens, Captain Peter, (A) *Narvik: Battles in the Fjords,* Ian Allan, 1974. (B) *Night action: MTB Flotilla at War,* Peter Davies, 1974.

Doenitz, Grand Admiral K., *Memoirs: Ten Years and Twenty Days,* Weidenfeld and Nicolson, 1958.

Dollmann, E., *The Interpreter,* Hutchinson, 1967.

Dourlein, P., *Inside North Pole,* William Kimber, 1953.

Dulles, Allen, (A) ed. by *Great True Spy Stories,* Collins. (B) *The Secret Surrender,* Weidenfeld and Nicolson, 1967.

Ehrlich, Blake, *The French Resistance,* Chapman & Hall, 1966.

Evans, J., *Confessions of a Special Agent,* Robert Hale, 1951.

Farago, Ladislas, (A) *War of Wits,* Hutchinson, 1956. (B) *The Broken Seal,* Arthur Barker, 1967. (C) *The Game of the Foxes,* Hodder & Stoughton, 1972.

Foot, M. R. D., *SOE in France,* H.M.S.O., 1966.

Foote, Alexander, *Handbook for Spies,* Museum Press, 1953.

Ford, Corey, *Donovan of the OSS,* Robert Hale, 1971.

Fourcade, Marie-Madeleine, *Noah's Ark,* George Allen & Unwin, 1973.

Frank, Wolfgang, *The Sea Wolves,* George Mann, 1973.

Franklin, Charles, *Spies of the Twentieth Century,* Odhams Press, 1967.

Fuller, Jean Overton, *The German Penetration of SOE,* William Kimber, 1975.

Ganier-Raymond, P., *The Tangled Web,* Arthur Barker, 1968.

Garlinski, Jozef, *Poland, SOE and the Allies,* George Allen & Unwin, 1969.

Gehlen, General R., *The Gehlen Memoirs,* Collins, 1972.

Giskes, H. J., *London Calling North Pole,* William Kimber, 1953.

Gramont, Sanche de, *The Secret War,* Andre Deutsch, 1962.

Green, J. M., *From Colditz in Code,* Robert Hale, 1971.

Gretton, Vice-Admiral Sir Peter, *Crisis Convoy,* Peter Davies, 1974.

Hagen, Louis, *The Secret War for Europe,* Macdonald, 1968.

Haldane, R. A., *The Hidden World,* Robert Hale, 1976.

Hamilton-Hill, Donald, *SOE Assignment,* William Kimber, 1973.

Haswell, Jock, *British Military Intelligence,* Weidenfeld and Nicolson, 1973.

Haukelid, Knut, *Skis Against the Atom,* Fontana, 1973.

Higgins, Trumbull, *Hitler and Russia,* Macmillan, 1966.

Hinchley, Colonel V., *Spy Mysteries Unveiled,* Harrap, 1963.

Hoehne, H., *Codeword Direktor,* Secker and Warburg, 1971.

Hoehne, H. & Zolling, H., *Network,* Secker and Warburg, 1972.

Hutton, J. Bernard, (A) *School for Spies,* Neville Spearman, 1961. (B) *Women Spies,* William Allen, 1971.

Hyde, H. Montgomery, *The Quiet Canadian,* Hamish Hamilton, 1962.

Ind, Colonel Allison, *A History of Modern Espionage,* Hodder and Stoughton, 1965.

Irving, David, *Breach of Security,* William Kimber, 1968.

Kahn, David, *The Code Breakers,* Sphere Books, 1973.

Kennedy, Major-General Sir John, *The Business of War,* Hutchinson, 1957.

Kesselring, Field Marshal A., *A Solidier's Record,* William Kimber, 1953.

Kilpatrick, Sir Ivone, *The Inner Circle,* Macmillan, 1959.

Kirkpatrick, Lyman B., *Captains Without Eyes,* Ruper Hart-Davis, 1970.

Leahy, Fleet Admiral W., *I Was There,* Gollancz, 1950.

Leasor, J. & Hollis, General Sir Leslie, *War at the Top,* Michael Joseph, 1959.

Leverkuehn, P., *Germany's Military Intelligence,* Weidenfeld and Nicolson, 1954.

Lockhart, Sir Robert Bruce, *Comes the Reckoning,* Putnam, 1957.

Lucas, Norman, *The Great Spy Ring,* Arthur Barker, 1966.

Macintyre, Captain D., (A) *The Battle of the Atlantic,* B. T. Batsford, 1961. (B) *U-boat Killer,* Corgi, 1976.

Macksey, Major K., *Crucible of Power,* Hutchinson, 1969.

Martens, A., *The Silent War,* Hodder and Stoughton, 1961.

Masson, Madeline, *Christine,* Hamish Hamilton, 1965.

Masterman, J. C., *The Double-Cross System,* Yale University Press, 1972.

McLachlan, D., *Room 39: Naval Intelligence in Action, 1939-45,* Weidenfeld and Nicolson, 1968.

Merrilees, W., *The Short Arm of the Law,* John Long, 1966.

Millar, G., *Maquis,* Portway, 1945.

Mohn, U. & Sellwood, A. V., *Atlantis: the Story of a German Surface Raider,* Hutchinson, 1972.

Moore, Tyler and Waller, Martha, *Cloak and Cipher,* Harrap, 1965.

Moravec, General, *Master of Spies,* Bodley Head, 1975.

Morgan, W. A., *Spies and Saboteurs,* Gollancz, 1955.

Morison, Rear-Admiral Samuel E., *History of U.S. Naval Operations in World War II*, Little, Brown and Co., Boston, 1964.

Moss, W. S., *A War of Shadows*, Boardman, 1952.

Moysich, L. C., *Operation Cicero*, Wingate-Barker, 1969.

Norman, Bruce, *Secret Warfare*, David and Charles, 1973.

Pack, Captain S. W. C., *Night Action off Matapan*, Ian Allen, 1972.

Page, Bruce; Leitch, David; and Knightley, Philip, *Philby: the Spy Who Betrayed a Generation*, Andre Deutsch, 1968.

Pape, Richard, *Boldness be my Friend*, Elek, 1953.

Papen, Franz von, *Memoirs*, Andre Deutsch, 1952.

Pawle, G., *The Secret War*, Harrap (White Lion edition), 1972.

Perrault, G., *The Red Orchestra*, Arthur Barker, 1967.

Piekalkiewicz, Janusz, *Secret Agents, Spies and Saboteurs*, David and Charles, 1974.

Piquet-Wicks, E., *Four in the Shadows*, Jarrolds, 1957.

Popov, Dusko, *Spy/Counter-Spy*, Panther Books, 1976.

Porten, E. P. von der, *The German Navy in World War II*, Arthur Barker, 1969.

Pratt, Fletcher, *Secret and Urgent*, Robert Hale, 1939.

Purdy, Anthony and Sutherland, Douglas, *Burgess and Maclean*, Secker and Warburg, 1963.

Raeder, Grand Admiral E., *Struggle for the Sea*, William Kimber, 1959.

Reitlinger, G., *The House Built on Sand*, Weidenfeld and Nicolson, 1960.

Ribbentrop, J. von, *The Ribbentrop Memoirs*, Weidenfeld and Nicolson, 1954.

Robertson, Terence, *Dieppe: the Shame and the Glory*, Pan books, 1965.

Roskill, Captain S. W., *The War at Sea*, H.M.S.O.

Rowan, R. W. and Deindorfer, R. G., *Secret Service*, William Kimber, 1969.

Salisbury, Harrison, *The Siege of Leningrad*, Secker and Warburg, 1969.

Schellenberg, W., *Memoirs*, ed. and translated by Louis Hagen, Andre Deutsch, 1956.

Schmidt, P., *Hitler's Interpreter*, Macmillan, 1951.

Schofield, Vice-Admiral B. B., *The Russian Convoys*, B. T. Batsford, 1964.

Schofield, Vice-Admiral B. B., and Martyn, Lieut-Commander L. F., *The Rescue Ships*, Blackwood, 1968.

Seth, Ronald, *Anatomy of Spying*, Arthur Barker, 1961.

Shankland, P. & Hunter, A., *Malta Convoy*, Collins, 1960.

Sillitoe, Sir Percy, *Cloak Without Dagger*, Quality Book Club.

Slessor, Marshal of the RAF Sir John, *The Central Blue*, Cassel, 1956.

Smith, Peter C., *Convoy PQ18, Arctic Victory*, New English Library, 1975.

Stead, P. J., *Second Bureau*, Evans Bros, 1959.

Strong, Major General Sir Kenneth, *Men of Intelligence*, Cassel, 1970.

Sweet-Escott, Bickham, *Baker Street Irregular*, Methuen, 1965.

Trevor-Roper, Hugh, *The Philby Affair*, William Kimber, 1968.

Tute, Warren; Costello, John; Hughes, Terry, *D-Day,* Sidgwick and Collins, 1974.

Upton, A., *Finland 1939-40,* Davis-Poynter, 1974.

Vansittart, Lord, *Lessons of my Life,* Hutchinson, 1947.

Walker, D. E., *Lunch with a Stranger,* Wingate, 1957.

Warner, O., *Marshal Mannerheim and the Finns,* Weidenfeld and Nicolson, 1967.

Waterfield, G., *Professional Diplomat: Sir Percy Loraine,* John Murray, 1973.

Whaley, Barton, *Codeword Barbarossa,* M.I.T., 1973.

Wheeler-Bennett, Sir John, *The Nemesis of Power,* Macmillan, 1954.

Whitwell, John, *British Agent,* William Kimber, 1966.

Wighton, Charles, *The World's Greatest Spies,* Odhams Press, 1962.

Wingate, Sir Ronald, *Lord Ismay,* Hutchinson, 1970.

Winterbotham, Group Captain F. W., *The Ultra Secret,* Weidenfeld and Nicolson, 1974.

Winton John, ed by, *Freedom's Battle: the War at Sea, 1939-45,* Hutchinson, 1967.

Wise, D. and Ross, T. B., *The Espionage Establishment,* Jonathan Cape, 1968.

Woodroofe, Commander T., *The Battle of the Atlantic,* Faber and Faber, 1965.

Young, Brigadier P., *Decisive Battles of the Second World War,* Arthur Barker, 1967.

Calvocoressi, P., Three broadcasts about the Enigma cipher, on 18th and 25th January and 1st February 1977, reproduced in the *Listener* (20th and 27th January and 3rd February, 1977).

References

Where no page number is given, reference is to the general theme of the book; reference to Calvocoressi are to his talks on BBC radio. Where the name of an author is followed by two figures in Roman type, the first refers to the number of the volume and the second to a separately produced part of it. The letters R.A.H. refer to the author's personal knowledge and experience of matters which have either not been covered or only partially covered in other sources.

CHAPTER ONE

1 Farago (A), p. 74
2 Cookridge (C), p. 8
3 Foot, p. 105
4 Whitwell (Introduction by Muggeridge)
5 Winterbotham, p. 74
6 R.A.H.
7 Calvocoressi
8 Ibid
9 Cookridge (*Daily Telegraph Supplement,* 23rd July 1976)
10 Schellenberg, p. 228
11 Masterman, p. 1
12 Farago (C), p. 415
13 Irving, p. 32 (Introduction by D. C. Watt)
14 Ibid
15 Farago (C), p. 416
16 Robertson, pp. 152-4
17 Tute, Costello and Hughes, p. 85
18 Farago (B), p. 78
19 Calvocoressi
20 R.A.H.
21 Winterbotham, p. 63
22 Ciano's diplomatic papers, p. 378
23 Collier, p. 491
24 Popov, p. 8
25 Gretton, p. 171
26 Roskill II, p. 208
27 Farago (C), p. 567
28 Hinchley, P. 230
29 Farago (C), p. 434
30 Colvin
31 Hoehne and Zolling, p. 298
32 Winterbotham, p. 3
33 Ibid, p. 191
34 Haldane, pp. 162, 163
35 Tute, Costello & Hughes, p. 83
36 Green

CHAPTER TWO

There is a fine choice of books well worth reading. Captain Roskill's official history in three volumes (Volume III in two parts) is a momentous work. The two books by Captain Macintyre are particularly informative. Those by Vice-Admiral Gretton and Vice-Admiral Schofield are also strongly recommended, and so is Rear-Admiral Creighton's book; and on Naval Intelligence McLachlan and Beesly. Commander Woodroofe's little book is excellent with a map showing the sinkings of surface vessels and U-boats. Rear-Admiral Morison (a writer-turned sailor, not the other way about) is most informative on the part played by the US Navy. Doenitz is thorough, detailed and long; the works of von der Porten and Frank (one of the earliest post-war writers on this subject) are of considerable interest. I found it often difficult to select from authorities for references.

1   Frank, p. 26
2   Doenitz, p. 56
3   Dickens, p. 13
4   Roskill III, Part II, p. 479
5   Arnold-Forster, p. 85
6   Schofield and Martyn, p. xix
7   Macintyre (B), p. 126
8   Cresswell, p. 67n
9   Macintyre (B), p. 111
10 Frank, p. 138
11 Avon, p. 390
12 Gretton, p. 22
13 Cresswell, p. 67
14 Macintyre (A), p. 13
15 Gretton, p. 25
16 Morison, p. 106
17 Macintyre (B), p. 36
18 Ibid, p. 37
19 Creighton, p. 166
20 Ibid, p. 140
21 Macintyre (A), p. 44
22 Creighton, p. 95
23 Macintyre (B), p. 116
24 Ibid, p. 17
25 Pawle, p. 25
26 Macintyre (B), p. 56
27 Macintyre (A), p. 30

28 McLachlan, p. 77
29 Deacon (A), p. 303
30 Morison, pp. 104, 105
31 Cunningham, p. 334
32 Morison, p. 103
33 McLachlan, p. 82
34 Ibid
35 Frank, p. 32
36 Von der Porten, p. 42
37 Macintyre (A), p. 31
38 Beesly, p. 61
39 McLachlan, p. 89
40 Macintyre (A), p. 29
41 Ibid, p. 62
42 Von der Porten, p. 180
43 Roskill I, p. 615
44 McLachlan, p. 391
45 Irving, p. 169
46 Ibid, p. 168
47 Ibid, p. 42
48 Frank, p. 36
49 Schellenberg, p. 117
50 Leverkuehn, p. 83
51 Dickens, p. 57
52 Ibid, p. 50
53 McLachlan, p. 85
54 Roskill I, p. 267

55 Beesly, pp. 61, 74n
56 Ibid, p. 64
57 Winterbotham, p. 84
58 Ibid
59 Whitwell, p. 100
60 Von der Porten, p. 174
61 Irving, p. 167
62 Ibid, also Roskill I, p. 267
63 Irving, p. 167
64 Mohr and Sellwood, pp. 127, 128
65 Irving, p. 167
66 McLachlan, p. 93
67 Doenitz, p. 325
68 McLachlan, p. 83
69 Cunningham, p. 592
70 Kahn, p. 269
71 Frank, p. 68
72 Macintyre (B), p. 105
73 Frank, pp. 68, 69
74 Ibid, p. 46
75 Woodroofe, p. 30
76 Macintyre (B), p. 30
77 Macintyre (A), p. 77
78 Irving, p. 172
79 McLachlan, p. 84
80 Cresswell, p. 61
81 Irving, p. 173
82 Von der Porten, p. 178
83 Ibid, p. 179
84 Frank, p. 120
85 Ford, p. 151
86 McLachlan, p. 83
87 Frank, p. 169
88 Von der Porten, p. 186
89 Cunningham, p. 553
90 McLachlan, p. 85
91 Frank, p. 92
92 Von der Porten, pp. 183-185
93 McLachlan, p. 89
94 Roskill I, p. 485
95 Von der Porten, p. 188
96 Roskill II, p. 111
97 Roskill I, p. 485

98 Woodroofe, p. 94
99 Macintyre (B), p. 172
100 Ibid, p. 106
101 Frank, p. 131n
102 Shankland and Hunter, p. 53
103 Cunningham, pp. 258, 259, 267
104 Schofield, p. 208
105 Leasor and Hollis, p. 140
106 Schofield, p. 29
107 Roskill II, p. 119
108 Cunningham, p. 617
109 Shankland and Hunter, p. 28
110 Hoehne, p. 144
111 McLachlan, p. 86
112 Roskill II, p. 367
113 Winterbotham, pp. 70, 94, 97
114 Frank, p. 106
115 Calvocoressi
116 Beesly, p. 177
117 Doenitz, p. 325
118 Winterbotham, pp. 84, 85
119 Beesly, pp. 33, 53
120 McLachlan, p. 84
121 Farago (C), p. 426
122 Macksey, p. 55
123 Raeder, p. 229
124 Roskill, III, II, p. 479
125 Roskill II, p. 208
126 McLachlan, p. 84
127 Roskill II, p. 376
128 Gretton, p. 24
129 Roskill III, I, p. 55
130 Cunningham, p. 625
131 Roskill III, I, p. 50
132 McLachlan, p. 85
133 Winterbotham, p. 21
134 Doenitz, p. 489
135 Von der Porten, p. 193
136 Gretton, p. 159
137 Roskill III, I, p. 315
138 Ibid, p. 53
139 Gretton, p. 171

CHAPTER THREE

Of the books on Russian espionage, Professor Dallin's is, in my view, outstanding. Deacon and Cookridge have both written histories of the Russian secret services, and Wise and Ross and Rowan and Deindorfer have also provided material, all of them informative. The details of training Russian agents are taken mainly from two books by Bernard Hutton. Those who want to pursue the construction of Russian ciphers and their intricacies are referred to David Kahn's massive *The Code Breakers,* the classic history of ciphers and codes and their unravelment. The original edition, published by Weidenfeld and Nicolson, is a *magnum opus:* notes on sources of information account for over 160 pages. The shorter edition (to which my page references apply) excludes notes on sources.

1   Dallin, p. 71
2   Lt-Col M. M. Haldane to the author
3   Farago (C), p. 473
4   Farago (A), p. 141
5   Kirkpatrick, p. 29
6   Whaley, p. 66
7   Hoehne, p. 33
8   Ibid, p. 36
9   Ibid, p. 39
10 Whitwell, pp. 20, 131, 220
11 Cookridge (C), p. 9
12 Hagen, p. 18
13 Cookridge (E), p. 97
14 Hoehne, p. 38
15 Hutton (A), pp. 52-65
16 Wise and Ross, p. 38
17 Seth, p. 87
18 Piekalkievicz, pp. 35, 36
19 Dallin, p. 269
20 Hutton (B), p. 106
21 Ibid, p. 26
22 Seth, p. 74
23 Wise and Ross, p. 15
24 Cookridge (C), p. 268
25 Hutton (A), p. 15
26 Farago (A), p. 142
27 Lucas, p. 104
28 Farago (C), p. 284
29 Masterman, p. 190
30 Ibid, p. 15
31 Ibid, p. 188
32 Hutton (A), p. 15
33 *Daily Telegraph* (10th, 11th March 1976)
34 Hutton (B), p. 119
35 Ibid, p. 41
36 Kahn, pp. 368, 369
37 Ibid, p. 216

CHAPTER FOUR

Hoehne's book is thorough and a classic history of the Rote Kapelle, but Piekalkievicz (whose book is full of excellent illustrations) and Perrault, both of whom interviewed participants, have provided most interesting contributions. So indeed have Dallin and Whaley whose *Codeword Barbarossa* is concentrated on the German preparations for the attack on Russia. Salisbury writes comprehensively on the siege of Leningrad, and Upton provides an excellent review of the Russian-Finnish war.

1 Foote, p. 45
2 Whaley, p. 98
3 Schellenberg, p. 329
4 Dallin, p. 152
5 Perrault, p. 16
6 Piekalkiewicz, p. 168
7 Perrault, p. 39
8 Hoehne, p. 44
9 Schellenberg, p. 326
10 Rowan and Deindorfer, p. 630
11 Hoehne, p. 147
12 Rowan and Deindorfer, p. 630
13 Hoehne, p. 114
14 Ibid, p. 42
15 Ibid, p. 43
16 Whitwell, p. 127
17 Salisburgy, p. 62n
18 Whaley, p. 21
19 Ibid, p. 109
20 Schellenberg, p. 323
21 Perrault, p. 56
22 Piekalkiewicz, p. 175
23 Hoehne, pp. 80, 81; Dallin, p. 153; Piekalkiewicz, p. 175
24 Perrault, p. 493
25 Ibid, p. 110
26 Hoehne, p. 83
27 Ibid, pp. 149, 150
28 Upton, pp. 53, 152
29 Warner, p. 170
30 Waterfield, p. 255
31 Salisbury, pp. 446, 575
32 Wingate, p. 65
33 Ibid, p. 66
34 Kirkpatrick, p. 164
35 Schellenberg, p. 323
36 Perrault, p. 110
37 Piekalkiewicz, p. 177
38 Schellenberg, p. 325
39 Perrault, p. 285
40 Hagen, p. 18
41 Cookridge (C), p. 7
42 Piekalkiewicz, p. 178
43 Schellenberg, p. 327
44 Ibid, p. 329
45 Leverkuehn, p. 183
46 Hoehne, p. xxviii
47 Ibid, p. 147
48 Perrault, p. 78
49 Dallin, p. 151
50 Hoehne, p. 236
51 Rowan and Deindorfer, pp. 630-1

CHAPTER FIVE

Alexander Foote's book may be considered the principal guide, he himself being one of the chief characters in the Swiss network, and his material is well set out. Both Dallin and Piekalkiewicz reveal original contributions; Dallin's book is beautifully written and Piekalkiewicz provides some interesting material. Hoehne includes a true example of one of Punter's enciphered signals. Carell's *Scorched Earth* is a detailed history of the way on the Eastern front and he devotes space to explaining the precautions taken by Hitler's security service against illicit transmission and comments on Lucy's transmissions; my references are all to Volume II of that work.

1 Foote, p. 77
2 Dallin, p. 187
3 Ibid, p. 198
4 Ibid, p. 210
5 Muggeridge (The *Observer*, 8th January 1967)
6 Foote, p. 45
7 Ibid, p. 166
8 Ibid, p. 27
9 Muggeridge (The *Observer*, 8th January 1967)
10 Foote, p. 75
11 Ibid
12 Dallin, p. 195
13 Foote, p. 98
14 Avon, p. 336
15 Foote, p. 110
16 Carell (A), 2, pp. 99ff
17 Wingate, p. 66
18 Arnold-Forster, p. 169
19 Piekalkiewicz, p. 209
20 Carell (A), 2, p. 21
21 Ibid, p. 103
22 Ibid, p. 64

23 Ibid, p. 93
24 Dollmann, p. 157
25 Piekalkiewicz, p. 208
26 Carell (A), 2, pp. 109, 110
27 Piekalkiewicz, p. 223
28 Dallin, p. 214
29 Foote, p. 142
30 Dallin, pp. 197, 198
31 Norman, p. 150
32 Piekalkiewicz, p. 223
33 Foote, p. 75
34 Carell (A), 2, p. 112
35 Gehlen, p. 86
36 Carell (A), 2, p. 112
37 Foote, p. 29
38 Carell (A), 2, p. 113
39 Accoce and Quet
40 Muggeridge (The *Observer*, 8th January 1967)
41 Kahn, p. 367 (p. 649 in the full edition)
42 Cadogan, p. 159
43 Carell (A), p. 111

CHAPTER SIX

Deakin and Storry's history of this phase of the Russian espionage service is detailed and fully documented.

1 Whaley, p. 71
2 Deakin and Storry, p. 115
3 Farago (A), p. 138
4 Deakin and Storry, p. 196
5 Ibid, p. 216

6 Schellenberg, p. 180
7 Deakin and Storry, p. 255
8 Ibid, p. 324
9 Ibid, p. 277

CHAPTER SEVEN

For the more advanced readers Kahn is the authority on technical aspects of Japanese ciphers; but Bruce Norman provides an excellent beginner's guide to understanding how Purple worked. Kirkpatrick has some shrewd comments to make, particularly on keeping the secret of breaking Purple confined to a small handful of people at the top. Winterbotham tells of the use of the key to Enigma in the war against Japan, both on land and at sea.

1 Kahn, p. 71
2 Farago (B), p. 59
3 Ibid, p. 58
4 Norman, pp. 114-16
5 Kahn, p. 407
6 Ibid, p. 394
7 Farago (B), pp. 79, 80
8 Kahn, p. 26
9 Farago (B), p. 99
10 Ibid, p. 103
11 Kahn, p. 11
12 Farago (B), p. 253
13 Churchill, W. S., p. 532
14 Kirkpatrick, p. 88
15 Ibid, pp. 89, 90
16 Kahn, p. 42
17 Popov, pp. 143-78
18 Kahn, p. 330
19 Ibid, p. 328
20 Winterbotham, pp. 168-76
21 Ibid, p. 175
22 Ibid, p. 176
23 Kahn, p. 335
24 Winterbotham, p. 176
25 Ibid, p. 106
26 Haldane, p. 112
27 Kahn, p. 5

CHAPTER EIGHT

There is a wide variety of contributors. Whitwell's book well repays reading. Ford, Whaley, Cookridge, Deacon, Seth and Murphy all have made valuable contributions. Masterman's story of how MI5 "turned" German spies is out on its own, supported by a book of character by Popov. Moysich tells the story of "Operation Cicero". Various others have also contributed. As always, Kahn remains the authority on the breaking of ciphers and codes. While Schellenberg's memoirs contain a good deal of oily "whitewash" and must therefore be read with considerable reservations, they include certain interesting and acceptable contributions.

1 Irving, pp. 24, 29 (Introduction by D. C. Watt)
2 McLachlan, p. 187
3 Irving, p. 31 (Introduction by D. C. Watt)
4 Dahlerus, p. 106
5 Irving, p. 33 (Introduction by D. C. Watt)
6 Ciano's diary, p. 239
7 Deacon (A), p. 335

8 Whitwell, p. 59
9 Ford, p. 283
10 Warner, p. 186
11 Ibid, p. 216
12 Ford, p. 284
13 Upton, p. 53
14 Smith, pp. 129-30 (referring to *Im Rucken des Reindes* by Jukka L. Makela)
15 Whaley, p. 153 (referring to Admiral Maugeri's *From the ashes of disgrace*, published by Reynal and Hitchcock, N.Y., 1948)
16 Montgomery Hyde, pp. 105-7
17 Cadogan, p. 427
18 Whitwell, p. 92
19 Farago (A), p. 189
20 Norman, p. 124
21 Carell (B), pp. 213, 227
22 Norman, p. 125
23 Delmer, p. 30
24 Ind, p. 215
25 Kahn, p. 239
26 Norman, p. 129
27 Ciano's diary, pp. 299, 372, 445, 483, 496, 499, 502, 538, 540, 542, 546
28 Whitwell, p. 113
29 Cadogan, p. 427
30 Whitwell, p. 194
31 Haldane, p. 84
32 Foote, p. 94
33 Farago (C), p. 472
34 Ibid, p. 473
35 Ibid
36 Seth, pp. 183-85
37 Ford, p. 156
38 R.A.H.
39 Deacon (A), p. 374
40 Moore and Waller, p. 81
41 Murphy, p. 78
42 Whaley, p. 167
43 McLachlan, p. 85

44 Macksey, p. 55
45 Winton, p. 262
46 Wingate, p. 84
47 Hamilton-Hill, p. 55
48 Farago (C), p. xiv
49 Leverkuehn, p. 142
50 Ibid, pp. 198, 199
51 Hoehne and Zolling, p. 27
52 Schellenberg, p. 393
53 Moysich, p. 70
54 Schellenberg, p. 419
55 Gehlen, p. 238
56 Moysich, p. 184
57 Irving, p. 175
58 Schellenberg, p. 390
59 Cadogan, p. 584
60 Ford, p. 285
61 Page, Leitch and Knightley, pp. 15-23 (Introduction by John le Carré)
62 Ibid, p. 213
63 Cookridge (B), p. 50
64 Ibid, p. 46
65 Page, Leitch and Knightley, p. 77
66 Cookridge (D), pp. 64-65
67 Cookridge (B), p. 105
68 Waterfield, p. 262
69 Whaley, p. 157
70 Ciano's diary, p. 239
71 Farago (C), p. 341
72 Cookridge (D), p. 123
73 Cookridge (B), pp. 109, 110
74 Popov, p. 230
75 Dallin, p. 12
76 Masterman
77 Popov, p. 108
78 Masterman, p. 73
79 Ibid, p. 53n
80 Popov, p. 157
81 Ibid, p. 215
82 Deacon, p. 336
83 R.A.H.

CHAPTER NINE

Beyond question Cookridge's work *Inside SOE* is an outstanding, detailed and comprehensive history, the author having consulted French, Dutch and other participants. Foot, the official historian, is concerned with operations only in France; though his book is otherwise comprehensive, he has less to say than Cookridge about the signal systems used. On the single operation of paramount importance, the destruction of Germany's heavy water supply, the Norwegian, Haukelid, is the authority at first hand, and I have drawn principally from his excellent book. Dalton's memoirs include a useful summary of the main achievements of SOE. Others, in particular Buckmaster, Hamilton-Hill, Cox, Walker, Ganier-Raymond, Piquet-Wicks and Sweet-Escott, all provide original and interesting contributions from personal service. Piekalkiewicz deals mostly with the training of agents and is excellently informed on that subject.

1   Buckmaster, p. 127
2   Butler, J. R. M., VIII, II, p. 517
3   Chandos, p. 239
4   Tute, Costello and Hughes, p. 5 (Introduction by Earl Mountbatten)
5   Whitwell, pp. 26, 220
6   Cookridge (B), p. 92
7   Hamilton-Hill, p. 64
8   Piekalkiewicz, p. 50
9   Haukelid, p. 44
10 Ford, pp. 230, 231
11 Deacon (A), p. 385
12 Churchill, P. (B), p. 281n
13 Whaley, p. 157
14 Foot, p. 68
15 Merrilees, pp. 139-44
16 Foot, p. 72
17 Ibid, p. 14
18 Ibid, p. 104
19 Perrault, p. 470
20 Foot, pp. 329, 330
21 Fuller, p. 178
22 Cookridge (A), p. 84
23 Piekalkiewicz, p. 61
24 Cookridge (A), p. 81
25 Merrilees, p. 142
26 Foot, p. 104
27 Sweet-Escott, p. 105
28 Cookridge (A), p. 403
29 Piekalkiewicz, p. 281
30 Cookridge (A), p. 405
31 Norman, p. 103
32 Ibid, p. 106
33 Ganier-Raymond, p. 94
34 Norman, p. 105
35 Cookridge (A), p. 435
36 Piekalkiewicz, p. 287
37 Ibid
38 Cookridge (A), p. 437
39 Ibid, p. 446
40 Ibid, p. 426
41 Ibid, p. 476
42 Ibid, p. 498
43 Ibid, p. 488
44 Ibid, p. 324n
45 Ibid, p. 578
46 Hamilton-Hill, p. 31
47 Dalton, pp. 374, 375
48 R.A.H.
49 Dalton, pp. 374, 375

50 Haukelid, p. 78
51 Piekalkiewicz, p. 279
52 Haukelid, p. 159n
53 Cookridge (A), p. 561
54 Hamilton-Hill, p. 89
55 Ibid, p. 104
56 Cox, p. 215
57 Sweet-Escott, p. 190
58 Dalton, p. 375

59 Moravec, p. 119
60 Garlinski, p. 29
61 Cookridge (A), p. 605
62 Ibid, p. 121
63 Dalton, p. 377
64 Foot, p. 339
65 Norman, pp. 159, 160
66 Dalton, p. 377
67 Ibid

CHAPTER TEN

1 Kahn, p. 269
2 Winterbotham, p. 1
3 Kahn, p. 224
4 Ibid, p. 266
5 Winterbotham, p. 143
6 R.A.H.
7 Winterbotham, pp. 187, 191
8 Roskill III, II, p. 388

9 Winterbotham, p. 44
10 Cunningham, p. 259
11 Calvocoressi and Wint,
    pp. 551-53
12 Beesly, p. 66n
13 McLachlan, p. 77
14 Piekalkiewicz, p. 222

Index

Hankey, Lord, 37
Harnack, A., 77, 79, 80, 81, 91, 92, 97, 98
Harriman, Averell, 69
Harris, Marshal of the RAF Sir Arthur, 38
Hassel, Ulrich von, 134, 181
Haukelid, Lieut-Colonel Knut, 175, 176
Hausamann, Major, 114, 115
Heavy water supply, German, 175, 176
Heath administration, 68
Hechalutz, 78
Hedgehog, 40
Heilmann, H., 80, 90
Hess, Rudolf, 25, 121
Heydrich, Reinhart, 30, 69, 84, 145, 178
High-speed transmission, 189
Himmler, H., 30, 145
Hinchley, Colonel V., 30n
Hiroshima, 176
Hitler, A., 15, 24, 25, 30, 31, 53, 64, 92, 93, 94, 100, 103, 113, 114, 121, 136n, 143, 145, 150, 151, 177, 185; decides to invade Denmark and Norway, 45, 176; anger at Torch, 58; attack on Russia, 84; orders but postpones Operation Citadel, 107; plans to flatten London with rockets, 174; ignorance of naval affairs, 32, 36, 46, 51, 61; plot to kill, 29, 114, 116; suicide, 109n.
Hoehne, H., 96, 98
Hoffmann-Scholz, Anna-Margaret, 83
Holland, fatal casualties among Jews, 172
Holmes, Sherlock, 157
Home Security, Ministry of, 154
Home Security War Room, 25n
Hoover, J. Edgar, 130
Horizontal communications, 70, 71
Hull, Cordell, 103
Hutton, J. B., 28, 67, 68

Iceland, 39
Icelandic alphabet, 75
Indiscretions, diplomatic, 21, 22, 134, 135, 181, 189
Information, Ministry of, 17n
International Brigade, 79, 102
International Labour Exchange, 101
Invisible ink, 153, 167, 178
Ironside, Field Marshal Lord, 136n
Irving, David, 28

Ile de France, 38
Italian dive-bombing, high quality of, 54; alphabet 75; Secret Service, 138; traditional type of ciphers, 188; surrender, 32, 109

Jacob, Berthold, 15
Japanese military ciphers, 128; inadequate standard of cryptanalysis, 126, 130; signals read by Americans, 130; legal procedure, 122; defiance of the rules of war, 129
Jellicoe, Admiral of the Fleet Earl, 37
Jodl, General A., 155
Joyce, William, 148, 152

KGB, 68
Kahn, David, 28, 182, 183
Kaltenbrunner, E., 146, 147
Katz, Hillel, 78, 79
Kauffmann, K., *see* ERDBERG, A.
Keitel, Field Marshal W., 24, 25, 91
Kell, Major-General Sir Vernon, 63n, 149, 150
Kennedy, Joseph, 141, 150, 152
Kent, Tyler, 152, 153
"Kern, Operation," *see* SPECIAL OPERATIONS EXECUTIVE
Kesselring, Field Marshal, A., 24, 132n, 139
Kharkov, 105
Kiel cipher, 70
Kimmel, Admiral H. E., 129
Kitabayashi, Tomo, 121
Klausen, Max, 119, 120, 122
Kluge, General G. von, 106, 108, 183
Koniev, Marshal I. S., 93
Konoye, Prince, 119, 122
Kowalewsky, Colonel J., 125, 126
Kruschev, N., 98
Kuckov, A., 80, 91, 97, 98
Kuehn, Ruth, 142
Kuibyshev, 88, 105
Kursk, Battle of, 91, 106, 107, 108, 109, 113, 115

Lauwers, H., 170, 171
"Lavatory, Operation," *see* SPECIAL OPERATIONS EXECUTIVE
League of Nations, 41
Leahy, Fleet Admiral W., 24
Le Carré, John, 148
Le Miracle de Professeur Wolmar, 90